# PEDRO
# ARRUPE

# PEDRO ARRUPE

## A HEART LARGER THAN THE WORLD

### BRIAN GROGAN, SJ

LOYOLA PRESS.
A JESUIT MINISTRY
Chicago

**LOYOLA**PRESS.
A JESUIT MINISTRY

www.loyolapress.com

Cover art credit: Society of Jesus
Back cover author photo: Piaras Jackson, SJ

ISBN: 978-0-8294-5520-5
Library of Congress Control Number: 2022935289

Printed in the United States of America.
22 23 24 25 26 27 28 29 30 31 Versa 10 9 8 7 6 5 4 3 2 1

*To all who find in Ignatian spirituality*
*a graced energy to serve the poor,*
*who are the friends of God.*

# Contents

# Introduction

The cause for the beatification of Pedro Arrupe, SJ, was launched in Rome by Fr. Arturo Sosa, SJ, superior general of the Society of Jesus, on February 5, 2019. A remarkable man in many ways, Arrupe played a central role in the Church after Vatican II, and his influence endures in the many who are fired by his idealism, vision, and way of life. He is widely recognized as one of the towering figures of the twentieth century, not only in ecclesiastical affairs but also in civil ones.

Born in Bilbao in 1907, Arrupe died in Rome in 1991. He had many life-shaping experiences: he witnessed miracles at Lourdes, which led him to join the Jesuit order in 1922; he was expelled from Spain with his fellow Jesuits in 1931; he began working in Japan in 1938, only to endure thirty-three days of solitary confinement on charges of espionage; he lived through Japan's military turmoil in World War II, including Pearl Harbor; and he was a first responder when the US dropped the atomic bomb on Hiroshima in 1945. He knew of the Holocaust, the rise of communism, the era of the Cold War, and the nuclear doctrine of mutually assured destruction. He lived through the endless regional conflicts and periodic genocides of the later twentieth century. None of these realities was lost on him; rather, they all shaped his heart's concerns.

In 1965 he was elected superior general of the Jesuits, then numbering thirty-six thousand men, and led them for sixteen challenging years as the Church grappled with implementing the decrees of the Second Vatican Council, held from 1962 to 1965. In 1975 he led the Jesuit order to affirm that the preaching of the gospel and the promotion of justice are inseparable, and in 1980, in response to the plight of Vietnamese refugees, called "boat people" at the time, he founded the Jesuit Refugee Service, which has since spread worldwide. Although Arrupe is a beacon of light and hope for many, during his life he was a sign of contradiction to not a few within the Jesuit order and the Vatican, including Pope St. John Paul II. He suffered a stroke in August 1981, after which he was marginalized and spent the last decade of his life in inner darkness and obscurity. He died in 1991.

Arrupe promoted the rediscovery of Ignatian spirituality, including the Spiritual Exercises and the art of discernment, both individual and corporate. Soon after taking over the governance of the Society, he asked God for the grace "to understand what the manifestation made to Ignatius means for us and for the Society today," and that grace was richly given to him. The restoration of the Ignatian style of discernment paved the way for the renewal of Jesuit life and the Jesuit mission to the world, which crystallized around the phrase "the faith that does justice." This mission means that the Society must always work for justice while proclaiming the gospel. Pedro, convinced by his twenty-seven years in Japan of the richness of the country's cultural diversity, promoted enculturation as a sign of respect for all those whom the Jesuits would try to help and as a dimension of the Good News. His startling vision for Jesuit alumni worldwide was that they be not only well-educated but engage creatively in the world as men and women for and with others.

The Church and society at large continue to be nourished in our times by the legacy of the Ignatian tradition as enriched by Pedro Arrupe. The current pope, Francis, also a Jesuit, is deeply rooted in this tradition, too. Fortunately for us, Arrupe has left behind a multitude of writings and addresses in which his values and inspiration shine through. He has influenced many religious congregations that in turn have touched the hearts of innumerable people who find themselves at home in a spirituality that emphasizes searching for and finding God in ordinary life. Arrupe's vision and enthusiasm for humankind have become embedded in

Catholic thinking, such that Peter-Hans Kolvenbach, who immediately succeeded him as superior general of the order, could say: "He no longer belongs to Jesuits only. He belongs to the whole Church: indeed, he belongs to the whole world."

Arrupe spent his life working to implement the reforms of the Second Vatican Council (known widely as Vatican II), and one sign of his enduring influence and the freshness of his thought is the fact that many Jesuit residences and works across the globe are named after him. But Pedro was always a simple man. A favorite line of his was "We Jesuits are poor men who just want to serve the people." Apart from his complete dedication to the Jesuit way of proceeding and a life of untiring prayer, he was a charming companion with an engaging sense of humor. Those who knew Pedro knew him as a tiny man who lived like a Church mouse, happy with the bare necessities of life. He also delighted in simple events: a poor man showing him the sunset, a woman in a Madrid tenement telling him the details of her family's daily life.

The range of his concerns was limitless, because he saw our world as God's. He prayed for the gift of prophecy, and he indeed had a prophetic gift to offer in response to the tragedies of humankind. In this way, Pedro shaped the lives of many people, both Jesuits and beyond, with optimism and vision that were in no way naïve but were based on the belief that the Lord cares for his people and calls generous hearts to help people in their need.

Eloquent and moving letters from all over the world confirm that Arrupe's reputation for holiness has been acknowledged in different sectors of the Church. After the Holy See's approval through the *nihil obstat* (or no objection), as well as the consent of the Italian Episcopal Conference and the absence of obstacles raised by the People of God, the session formally opening his cause for beatification took place at the Basilica of St. John Lateran on February 5, 2019, the twenty-eighth anniversary of his death.

The current superior general, Fr. Arturo Sosa, SJ, stated:

I am convinced that the person of Father Pedro Arrupe will inspire in Jesuits and in those [with] whom we partner in mission a greater desire for union and spiritual renewal, and that he will impel us to greater collaboration in the reconciliation of all things in Christ. He will guide us, under the Roman Pontiff, wherever the Spirit leads.[1]

# 1

## PEDRO'S SPIRITUALITY

### Encountering the Man

An encounter with Pedro Arrupe was for many people a dynamic and life-changing event. This was my own experience, and as you read these pages, I hope you find it to be true for yourself—you don't have to be a Jesuit or a believer to enjoy his company!

In the summer of 1981, I was a young priest between assignments and planning a mini-sabbatical when my provincial superior invited me to go on a short mission to Somalia. My poor knowledge of geography meant that I had to search for the exact location of that country that has faced so many challenges. The communist authorities had expelled all but four priests in 1974, and in 1981, the archbishop of

Mogadishu, who was later assassinated, wanted to test how Somalia's authorities might react to the return of priests. So he asked Pedro Arrupe, the Jesuits' superior general, to send him a man to find out how things stood, and the provincial sent me. The mission would be an opportunity, I was told, to do some fieldwork for the Jesuit Refugee Service (JRS), which Pedro had inaugurated only a year earlier, and like many of my companions, I was enthusiastic about the JRS. It was in such an unlikely situation that the seeds for this book were sown.

A weekly plane for Mogadishu left from Rome, so I flew there from Dublin, and one of Pedro's close advisers—an Irishman and a friend of mine—invited me to visit Pedro, who had had a devastating stroke two months earlier. Pedro had visited Ireland in 1967, and I had met him since: my task now was to cheer him with the news that the JRS was breaking new ground and to get his blessing for the enterprise. It was to be my sixth and final meeting with him.

In the darkened room where he was convalescing, I explained in stumbling Spanish where and why I was going. His eyes lit up: he half-raised himself from the couch, stuck out a trembling arm at me, and shouted "Go!" I had long thought of Pedro, with his frail body and broad smile, as a person in whom the Holy Spirit had unrestricted freedom of operation, so I took his command as from God, and go I did. His "Go!" energized me and kept me going in the scarier moments of that difficult trip, and it still does when I find myself backing away from difficulties. For example, as I write this very book, a niggling doubt assails me: *Who am I to try to convey to others the mystery of this man's extraordinary life?*

I begin this present enterprise by asking for Pedro's help, and his command "Go!" of thirty years ago in a dark Roman room echoes again for me. So far as I can, I shall let him speak for himself, often in abbreviated excerpts. The sources he has bequeathed to us are abundant and inspirational, and anecdotes about him still abound whenever older generations of Jesuits gather.

Arrupe's acceptance speech upon his election as superior general in 1965 began with a quotation from the book of Jeremiah. God had called Jeremiah out of obscurity 2,500 years ago to be a prophet: "Ah, Lord God! Truly I do not know how to speak." But God said, "You shall go to all to whom I send you, and you shall speak whatever I command you" (Jeremiah 1:6–7). "You shall go!" It seems to me that with his limitless enthusiasm, his "Go!" Pedro himself was always trying to respond to the Spirit. He spent his life coaxing people like me out of our comfort zones to do likewise. No one shaped my life more than he did, because from the moment he was elected general in 1965 he worked to radically reenergize the Society of Jesus, which I had joined as a teenager in 1954.

# The Density of God

Pedro was a tiny man with a great heart. Never threatening or dominating, he was always welcoming, and when he looked at you with his big eyes, you knew he had space in his heart for you. He was transparent: when writing on the person of Christ, he used the term *luminous transcendence* to refer to Jesus, and the same term could be applied to himself. Pedro radiated an inner glow; he had something of what Hindus speak of as "the density of God." Science says that humans are interconnected bundles of matter and energy, and theology adds that it is God who breathes that energy into us—and to me, Pedro verifies these things.

Jesus embodied a magnetism that made those sent to arrest him say, "Never has anyone spoken like this" (John 7:46); later his arrest squad fell to the ground before him (John 18:6). To be in Jesus' presence was life giving to those with openness of heart. Pedro, too, radiated an energy and hope that cannot easily be explained away. For years Br. Pedro Garcia was Arrupe's driver on his local trips around Rome. He recalls the following incident:

> If he didn't have to speak with someone else, he always sat up front beside me. And when he wanted to take advantage of the time to pray, he would first ask my permission. Perhaps the most important experience I had with him was the day one of the assistants had just told him that he

was leaving the order. A few minutes later, I took Arrupe someplace in the car. There was something special about him: not only was he not annoyed or worried but he transmitted a supernatural faith and peace. I don't know how to express what I felt, but I can say that at the hour of my death I will remember that half hour.[2]

Now that Pedro has passed beyond death, God's infinite energy has free play in him. "Resting in peace" is surely a weak description of how it must now be with him: I think of Pedro not simply as a fascinating figure of the past but as glowing even more brightly than he did when he lived among us, as energizing the rest of us and exercising an unobtrusive but enriching influence on our choices. We'll return to this idea later.

## A Man in Love

It is important from the outset to emphasize what made Pedro tick, lest the record of his outer struggles and achievements eclipse the "secret scripture" of his busy and eventful life. His spirituality—his life as he lived it out before God cannot be seen as an add on chapter to his biography. Rather, it informed his life from an early age and influenced all his adult choices. It was the air he breathed. His spirituality was profoundly centered on the three divine Persons, and this fact alone makes sense of all that transpired in his life.

While Pedro had a public side that delighted the media, he also had an array of consultants, an "inner cabinet," to advise him in private. Of these the main ones were the Father, the Son, and Holy Spirit, whom he met in his "back office," the small private chapel in Rome that he called his "cathedral." Each day he spent hours in conversation with them, and they also traveled with him, unobtrusive but always available, as he crisscrossed the globe. His words and actions emerged from time spent with this "inner cabinet"! He speaks of his little oratory as

> the fountain of incalculable power and dynamism for the whole Society, a place of inspiration, consolation and strength . . . where the Master's glance and mine cross each other, where one learns much in silence . . . The general would have the Lord all the time, every day, next to him, with just a partition between them.[3]

As if to help us to catch on to the power of the divine presence in his life, Pedro wrote a remarkable address in 1980, only a year before a stroke incapacitated him. Titled "The Trinitarian Inspiration of the Ignatian Charism," the address tells what went on in secret between God and Ignatius of Loyola, founder of the Jesuits in the sixteenth century. Ignatius tells us that he could not stop talking about the Trinity, which he describes as like the harmony of three musical keys, and he acknowledges that in his prayer and at Mass he was intimately in touch with the Trinity. Ignatius wrote a book on the Trinity that sadly has been lost; Pedro's address fills the gap, and it is a testament not only to Ignatius but also to Pedro's own personal spirituality.

In Pedro's enthusiastic style he reveals how he is caught into the encircling life of the Trinity. He is enraptured by the luminous mystery of the three Persons who dwell at the heart of all reality and who have kind purposes for all of humankind. For him, to be in touch with them was life itself, and so he tried to view every person he encountered, every situation and every decision, from a divine viewpoint. The three divine Persons steadily became his primary point of reference: he looked to them for support, guidance, and inspiration. In the Spiritual Exercises (101) Ignatius invites retreatants to sit with the three divine Persons as they contemplate their world in its need and decide how to respond. Retreatants are then to think over what to say to the three divine Persons and to beg for the grace to follow and imitate more closely our Lord, who has become human for them. Pedro did just this in his long daily hours of silent contemplation.

For Arrupe, only the dynamics of divine relationships give meaning to what goes on in the world. Given that God *is* community, he accepted that the divine project is to gather everyone and all things into loving relationships. So he waited on the three divine Persons, met them, was consoled by their company, and was illuminated and strengthened by the tasks they gave him. What mattered above all else to Pedro was to have the inner sense that he was acting—or enduring—according to their desire. This is what Ignatian consolation meant to him.

To illuminate the immense horizons of this perspective, which shaped the details of Pedro's life from youth onward, we will sketch in his own words his relationship with each person of the Trinity.

## The Hand of the Father

From his early years Pedro enjoyed a sustaining and intimate relationship with God as Father, which never faltered despite the severest trials. Even much later in his life, in his declining years, when he felt that he was "no use for anything," he acknowledged that "the most important thing in life is communicating with God."[4]

In 1977, with several others he celebrated his golden jubilee as a Jesuit. Recalling his early years in the Society, Pedro said with emotion that each of our personal histories has a thread running through it—and each thread is original and different:

> When we hear these personal histories, we perceive that something is left unsaid in all of them because it cannot be spoken: it is a personal secret that even the persons

themselves cannot fully perceive. This is the most truly interesting part, because it is what is most intimate, profound and personal. It is the close correlation between God who is love, and who loves each person in a different way, and the person who in the depth of their being gives a unique response, for there will be no other response like it in all of history. It is the secret of the marvelous trinitarian love that irrupts, when it so desires, into the life of each person in a way that is unexpected, inexpressible, irresistible, but at the same time marvelous and decisive.[5]

Pedro is speaking out of personal experience here, wrestling with that inexpressible factor, that ideal of ever-greater service that fueled his spirit as it did that of his great mentor, Ignatius of Loyola. He concludes simply: "I have the impression that my life is written in a single sentence: It has unfolded according to the will of God."[6]

He had a sense that the hand of God was at play in all the decisive turns, both positive and negative ones, that shaped his life. Reflecting on the elements of this enduring pattern he said:

My vocation to the Society of Jesus in the middle of my medical studies that so interested me; my vocation to Japan which superiors denied me for ten years while they prepared me to be a professor of moral theology; my presence in Hiroshima over which exploded the first atomic bomb; my election as general of the Society—these have been quite unexpected and abrupt events, but they have at the same time borne the mark of God so clearly that I have really considered them, and still consider them, as those irruptions whereby God's loving providence is pleased to manifest its presence and absolute dominion over each of us.[7]

After being incapacitated by a stroke, Pedro stated:

More than ever I find myself in the hands of God. This is what I have wanted all my life from my youth. But now there is a difference; the initiative is entirely with God. It is indeed a profound spiritual experience to know and feel myself so totally in God's hands.[8]

Pedro's dynamism was fired by a personal and living experience of falling in love with God. To describe the overpowering reality of God for him, we might borrow the lines of the Jesuit poet Gerard Manley Hopkins: "Thou mastering me / God, giver of breath and bread / . . . Lord of living and dead / . . . Dost thou touch me afresh? / Over again I feel thy finger and find thee."[9]

Again, as Ignatius speaks of himself as being "ablaze with God"—in fact, a recent biographer described him as "a man led by Another"—the same was true for Pedro, who would have made his own the line from the Renaissance poet Philip Sidney: "My true love hath my heart, and I have his." When celebrating his golden jubilee in the Society, Pedro remarked on his amazement and gratitude "not only for the privileged moments of my life, but above all for the uninterrupted and immeasurable graces I have received each day during the course of everyday life."[10]

## The Heart of the Son

The depth of Pedro's relationship with the Son of God is revealed across his writings, but especially when, in 1973, he strongly commended a renewed devotion to the Sacred Heart, which for various reasons was waning across the Society. While he accepts that the word *sacred* might be dropped, he describes the word *heart* as a primary word, packed with meaning and sentiment. For him, devotion to the Heart of Christ expresses the fundamental reality of being in love with he who is already limitlessly in love with us:

> It could be said that every line of the Gospel, every word of it, is throbbing with the boundless love of Christ, who is burning with love for each human being . . . The Word of God dwells in the innermost depths of our heart. Augustine (says): If you wish to love the whole Christ, you must open your heart wide. For . . . his presence extends to the whole world in his members, that is, in each human being.[11]

Speaking to the Son, he says:

I have discovered that the ideal of our way of acting is your way of acting. For this reason I fix my eyes on you. Give me that grace, that sense of you, your very heartbeat, so that I may live all of my life exactly as you did during your mortal life . . . Teach me your way of looking at people: as you glanced at Peter after his denial, as you penetrated the heart of the rich young man and the hearts of your female and male disciples. I would like to meet you as you really are, since your image changes those with whom you come into contact.[12]

In his later life Pedro recalled that when asked in a television interview, "Who is Jesus Christ for you?" the question took him by surprise. He answered it spontaneously:

For me Jesus Christ is everything . . . For me Jesus Christ is *everything*. . . . Take Jesus Christ from my life and everything would collapse, like a human body from which someone had removed the skeleton . . . The encounter with Jesus Christ is an essential condition for the apostolic life of a Jesuit. Without this love for Christ, the Society would no longer be the one that St. Ignatius founded, the Society of Jesus.[13]

## The Vision of the Holy Spirit

Pedro lived in close harmony with the Holy Spirit and composed prayers for the gift of discernment. His address "The

Trinitarian Inspiration of the Ignatian Charism" includes a prayer to see the world as God does:

> Grant me, O Lord, to see everything now with
>     new eyes,
> to discern and test the spirits
> that help me read the signs of the times,
> to relish the things that are yours, and to
>     communicate them to others.
> Give me the clarity of understanding that you gave
>     Ignatius.[14]

He lived by discernment because his abiding desire was to do whatever God wanted and at whatever cost. If he does not often mention the Spirit, it is because only with Vatican II did the long-eclipsed Spirit begin to feature explicitly in the worship, spirituality, and decision-making processes of the Church. But as a man accustomed to giving as many as four hours to prayer on even a busy day, he had a fine-tuned heart that searched endlessly for the presence of the Spirit in the signs of the times as they unfolded around him. Pedro was much like Ignatius, who, when faced with the challenges of his own times, asked in prayer: "What ought I do?" and tried to discern whether God were calling him to intervene, and if so, how. The spirituality of finding God in all things was not bounded by Ignatius's personal preconceptions or limited horizons—and the same can be said of Pedro.

Reflecting on his life on the occasion of his seventieth birthday, he affirms the power of the Spirit:

> There are historic moments—and a post-conciliar era is always such—in which the breakthrough of the Spirit produces such an impact in the world that it becomes like a city after an earthquake or a tornado . . . those houses with weaker foundations collapse, but that makes it possible to rebuild the city along more beautiful lines. These first years after Vatican II have left the impression in the Church of a "typhoon" that swept up in its path everything that was weak or obsolete. The Church has been aired out, . . . invigorated, and we can look to the future with great joy and breadth of spirit.[15]

## 2

## ALWAYS CHOOSING GOD

Discernment is the art of making choices. As mature persons, we often engage in discernment of one sort or another. In the Garden of Eden, Adam and Eve are depicted as having a basic decision to make: to choose in line with God's wishes for them or to go their own way. The Hebrew Scriptures tell of the constant battle between God's voice and human preferences, and the story goes badly because the human heart is unsteady and devious, and the concerns of God and others are easily eclipsed by personal desire.

Jesus' style is in sharp contrast to this because his heart is set unwaveringly on God: "I always do what is pleasing to him" (John 8:29). In every decision Jesus labors to do the wisest and most loving thing, and at whatever cost. So, when as Christians we want to know what God wants done, we are to put Christ and gospel values at the center of the process: this is the world of *Christian* discernment.

# The Language of the Heart

Ignatius of Loyola (1491–1556), who founded the Jesuits with a small group of companions in 1540, has left a rich legacy to the art of Christian discernment. In pondering his own choices, he found that he was being drawn in the direction that God had in mind for him, and he knew this through the experience of joy that was attached to one option rather than another. This experience might parallel the spontaneous sensitivity of a good person who wants to make only those choices that are in harmony with the preferences of a beloved other. We should, Ignatius says, permit the Creator to deal directly with the creature, and the creature directly with his Creator and Lord.[16]

Ignatius developed a deep interior sensitivity to the desires of God, which he named "consolation" as opposed to "desolation." He attended to the niggles, the trifling doubts, that accompany poorly made choices. "This *seems* good, but is it in fact coming from my own compulsions or evasions rather than from God?" He demands reflectiveness, and he sets the bar high:

> The love that moves and causes a person to choose must descend from above, that is, from the love of God, so

that before a person chooses they should perceive that the greater or less attachment for the object of their choice is solely because of their Creator and Lord.[17]

Arrupe made his own such guidelines for good decision-making as spelled out in the Exercises, the goal of which is to help a person become free in order to respond to the calls of God rather than the urgings of any selfish preferences. The overriding issue for Arrupe, then, was the question, What does God want? He spent his days consulting others, studying the issue at hand, using reason and imagination, listening well, and above all searching for the touch of God within his own heart. For Ignatius, the work of the good spirit in the human heart is quiet and gentle, "like a drop of water falling on a sponge," and to hear it, one must be silent within and expectantly await the whisper or gesture of God. Hence Pedro's long hours of prayer. Out of those hours, though, emerged a clarity about what he should do day by day as superior general. Because his myriad decisions would radically affect the lives of Jesuits and of many others, the labor of discernment was central to his life, and it brings us back to what we have explored of his Trinitarian spirituality, which was grounded in the real and messy world around him.

## Choices, Choices!

In regard to many choices, Arrupe had a clear and immediate vision of what to do. For example, he remarked that from the time of his entry into the Society of Jesus in 1927, he had a simple intuition of the love of Christ, which was enriched daily and became very fruitful for him. Two years later, in 1929, he noted that during his annual retreat he had a clear vision that his vocation was to be a missionary and that it would lead him to Japan.[18] Referring to an experience he had as a young Jesuit student, he said: "I saw everything clearly." Such statements recur throughout his life.[19] In regard to the option for justice, he stated during his sickness that even during the Second Vatican Council he had spoken about dialogue with the world. "At that time many of the council fathers were saying, 'What nonsense!' But I felt free. I knew: 'It is of God.'"[20]

Pedro frequently caught on to the divine meaning hidden in events and what God was asking of him in response. Thus, while a horrified world watched the mushroom cloud of the atomic bomb over Hiroshima, Pedro determined right away to put all available Jesuit resources into serving the wounded. In 1980, with millions of others, he observed Vietnamese refugees, known as "the boat people," fleeing from their country, but he immediately intuited that he should help them, and in that moment the seed of the Jesuit Refugee Service was sown, to which we will return later.

Although he was strongly intuitive, some decisions on what to do in response to pressing needs required longer gestation. We will look at the 1971 synod Justice in the World, which he attended and eloquently participated in as president of the Union of Superiors General. After it ended, he began to ponder how the Society should respond to its challenging message that "action on behalf of justice and participation in the transformation of the world are a constitutive dimension of the preaching of the gospel."[21]

Slowly, and after much consultation and prayer, he came to see that he should call a General Congregation to enable the Jesuits as a body to discern together what best to do in response to this radical call of the Church. In his retirement, he remarked: "We were beginning something new that would have great consequences."[22]

For Pedro, discernment was the essence of Jesuit identity. It was thus that he lived. One of his long-term assistants, the Irish Jesuit Cecil McGarry, stated:

I felt at home with him from the first moment I met him. When I was with him I felt somehow that I was in the presence of God, and that when I was talking with him God was always present as the third person, because he was so in touch with God. He was also intuitively in touch with the modern world. He knew where we were going and he was willing to work out how to get there. Also, he was a totally free man: he didn't care what people said about him as long as he was convinced that he was going in the right direction.[23]

One is reminded by this quote of the inscription that the Swiss psychiatrist Carl Jung placed above his front door: "Bidden or unbidden, God is present." Pedro believed this, too, and he made it his constant task to find God.

When sketching out the daily routine of the general, Ignatius wrote in 1540:

The general ought to employ the time which his health and energies allow him, partly with God, partly with his helpers, and partly with himself in reflecting privately and thinking out and deciding what should be done with the help and favour of God our Lord.[24]

From the beginning of his post as superior general, Pedro was convinced of the importance of communal discernment—hence his endless meetings, media interviews, and one-to-one encounters. On his sickbed twenty years later, he remarked of communal discernment: "That is old now; it is already something accepted. It is what Saint Ignatius would do today."[25]

# Contemplative in Action

A close companion of Ignatius, Jerónimo Nadal, coined the phrase "contemplatives, even when in action" to describe Ignatius's vision for the members of the Society. "But," a frustrated superior once confided to me, "the trouble with some of our guys is that all they're good for is contemplative *inaction!*"

Pedro, though, reclaimed the original charism of the Jesuits as illuminated by the light of the Second Vatican Council: he can be described as "a mystic with open eyes" because he gazed on our messy world—with its bombs, refugees, imprisonments, tortures, genocides, world wars, grinding poverty, clashes of ideologies—as God does. He was truly a contemplative in action: with God he looked at the world in all its joys and sorrows and tried to discern how God might want the Jesuit order to respond to the world's needs. He wanted only to follow the direction given by the Spirit, even if it led into uncertain ways and into errors. He encouraged his Jesuit companions to see with the eyes of Christ, go wherever the need was greatest, serve the faith, and promote justice—thus they would find God.

In 1978 there was a gathering in Rome of Jesuits elected to evaluate how the Society was implementing the groundbreaking fourth decree of the 32nd General Congregation (1974–1975), *The Faith That Does Justice*. Pedro's creativity led him to compose for the gathering his own version of the Church's ancient hymn to the Holy Spirit, "Veni, Creator Spiritus." His version draws its inspiration from Scripture and the personalities of salvation history. Some extracts convey its intensity, concreteness, and directness:

> Lord, I need your Spirit, that divine force that has transformed so many human personalities, making them capable of extraordinary deeds and extraordinary lives . . . The judges of Israel . . . simple sons of villagers, were changed by you, abruptly and completely . . . and felt themselves capable of . . . liberating a whole people . . .
>
> Give me those wondrous gifts that you lavished on your elect . . . wisdom and intelligence, counsel and strength . . . knowledge and fear of God . . .
>
> Give me what you gave the Prophets. Even if my little being protests, see me forced to speak by a supreme pressure . . . Give me the strength that kept *them* standing as they spoke to the people . . .
>
> Give me that Spirit that transformed weak Galilean fishermen into the columns of your Church and into apostles who gave through the holocaust of their lives the supreme testimony of their love for their brothers and sisters.
>
> Thus, this life-giving outpouring will be like a new creation, of hearts transformed, of a sensibility receptive to the voices of the Father, of a spontaneous fidelity to his

word . . . This then is what I pray, kneeling before the Father: *Come, Holy Spirit*.[26]

Arrupe's all-encompassing reliance on the Spirit was revealed when he was (frequently) asked, "Where is the Society going?" His answer was always along these lines:

Where God takes it! I don't know, but I do know one thing, that God is taking us somewhere. We are traveling safely, we are travelling with the Church that is guided by the Holy Spirit. I know that God is taking us to the promised land, his own land. He knows where it is: our job is simply to follow him.[27]

He was an optimist by nature, but the optimism displayed here came solely from the promise of Jesus: "Remember, I am with you always, to the end of the age" (Matthew 28:20). He could also use humor to disarm pessimists. When asked, as he frequently was, about the decline in vocations, he quipped: "Last man out, turn out the lights!"[28]

## A Demanding Love

Ignatius's goal was simply "to help others." Pedro's love also expresses itself in service. This is a mysticism not of solitary contemplation but of loving engagement. It is neither a disincarnate spiritualism nor a secular social activism. Instead, it is the exercise of pure charity toward God and toward one's neighbor. "Love is found in deeds rather than in words," as Ignatius tersely puts it.[29] Pedro acknowledges from his own experience its challenging quality:

> A demanding love it is, calling forth . . . a response of love and of service—service, which is itself love. This is the message of the very last paragraph of the Exercises: "The zealous service of God our Lord out of pure love should be esteemed above all" (370). In the Exercises we find terms and concepts which are logically reducible to one another: "the glory of God," for example, can be replaced by "the service of God." The same may be said of "praise" and "reverence." Only one term is final and irreducible to any other: *Love*.[30]

A demanding love it was for Pedro, especially in the ecclesial context. He was superior general during the turbulent post-conciliar years and the opening of Pope John Paul II's pontificate: the challenges that faced Pedro can be understood only in this context. Peter-Hans Kolvenbach, his immediate successor, stated at Pedro's funeral liturgy:

> Father Arrupe was tested in his love of the Church. His efforts to renew the Society in accord with the dynamic pace of Vatican II were met with the incomprehension of some and even painful interventions by the Church, which he loved with an Ignatian heart . . . He entered into the mystery of God's will, which sometimes imposes the

duty of suffering with loving humility at the hands of the Church. He dared to abandon old customs and habits in order to expose the Society, through spiritual discernment, to what God desired of it for Christ's mission in the heart of our world.[31]

Pedro saw this call to loving service as addressed not only to himself but also to those formed in Ignatian spirituality: "Nowadays the world does not need words but lives which cannot be explained except through faith and love for Christ's poor."[32] This is the heart of the man.

## Helping Those in Need

A key Ignatian dynamic is contained in the word *more* (Latin: *magis*). An umbrella term, it catches up the enthusiasm of the medieval code of chivalry and involves the sublimation of one's best desires and talents for the service of God and the world. The opposite of *magis* is half-heartedness, or mediocrity. Those imbued with this Ignatian dynamism see God as ever active, laboring in a changing world and inviting their collaboration. This openness to the freshly emerging will of God creates a restlessness that can be disconcerting for those who work with Jesuits, who may move on from already-excellent works and established institutions to what they believe to be a greater—even if seemingly unpromising—need.

Ignatius's desire was to help those who were neglected and in greater need than himself. His followers were meant to live out of an awesome grace that tilts them toward seeing the world with the eyes of Christ, loving it with his heart, and serving the world with his compassion. They would need discerning hearts as they edged their way along in uncharted territories. "The greater glory of God" thus became the Jesuit motto, and Ignatius and his companions called themselves "companions of Jesus" because in their lives, as in the life of Jesus, contemplation and action would fuse into one.

As a young man, Pedro was captivated by these Ignatian ideals. We see the *magis* operating throughout his life in his inner freedom and in his desire to be as available as possible to God. We see it in all these places:

- His choice for God's service, which entailed abandoning his medical studies and a potentially prestigious career
- His desire to serve in Japan, at the time the most difficult of mission fields
- His immediate response to the suffering of the inhabitants of Hiroshima
- His accepting of the challenge to lead the Jesuit order into an unknown future in the wake of the Second Vatican Council

- His offer to resign when his relations with Pope John Paul II reached a low ebb
- His struggle to remain positive through the dark years of his final illness, when he could do nothing but endure

## Trust in Providence

At Christmas in 1971 Arrupe wrote to his family, "One never knows what the new year will bring . . . but we can always be sure that God's constant aid and his loving, if at times inscrutable providence, will never fail us."[33]

He radiated inner tranquility, strength, and composure. As we explore the pressures from the world and the Church, and from within the Society, we come to realize the powerful inner resources Pedro had that enabled him to cope. For example, during the 32nd General Congregation, a serious misunderstanding arose between Pope Paul VI and Arrupe. It ended only when he was summoned by the pope, given pen and paper, and told to write down what Cardinal Benelli dictated to him. It was, he admitted later, one of the most humiliating experiences of his life. He was hurt especially by the attitude of the cardinal and burst into tears afterward when alone. But by the time he spoke to his waiting brethren, he had worked through his feelings and regained his composure. He then invited the delegates to concelebrate Mass and preached to them on the joy of obedience.[34]

Pedro lived with a high degree of imperturbability. He could be corrected, even criticized, but he did not hit back. His focus was on God, not himself. He was, in the best sense, "lost in God," so certain of God that accidental mishaps did not faze him. He often knew who his enemies were, but he received them graciously and was not cold with them; he seemed not to be fearful of them. There was nothing opaque in him, no apparent dark sanctum subject to the variations of moods that afflict the rest of us. He never struck a tone of self-concern or self-pity.

The Trappist monk Thomas Merton wrote:

> At the centre of our being is a point of nothingness, which is untouched by sin and by illusion, a point of pure truth, a point or spark which belongs entirely to God, which is never at our disposal, from which God disposes of our lives, which is inaccessible to the fantasies of our own mind or the brutalities of our own will. This little point of nothingness and of *absolute poverty* is the pure glory of God in us.[35]

This "pure glory" shines out more easily from some people than from others; it shone out in Jesus, who, when betrayed, bore his passion with loving patience. Pedro's "self" seemed to have been eclipsed by "the pure glory of God." He saw people as Francis of Assisi did—as images of God, "multiplied but not monotonous," in the words of G. K. Chesterton. Negativity had no visible place in his psychology: while he was constantly challenging his companions to live up to the call of Vatican II, in none of his writings do we find him blaming, scolding, judging, or condemning those who were lagging behind or making life difficult for him as leader. He was instead highly self-aware and received the sacrament of reconciliation regularly.

It is from this rich background and context that we can now turn to Pedro's life as it unfolded.

# 3

## EARLY YEARS, 1907–1938

### The Context

Pedro Arrupe's life spanned a century of two world wars and many other conflicts, as well as the Holocaust and genocides. But he also saw in his life the success of the women's suffrage movement and the birth of the United Nations, with its Universal Declaration of Human Rights, which applied to men and women. The atomic bomb destroyed Hiroshima and Nagasaki, and new technology equipped the great powers with enough weapons to destroy the world. But this period also brought space exploration, the landing on the moon, the first picture of Earth from space, the sense of our common home, and awareness that ours is not a static but an expanding universe. The first rumblings of ecological concern were heard in this time: the myth of progress and unlimited growth began to be challenged by writers such as Rachel Carson, who published her book *Silent Spring* in 1962. Shedding light into the darkness of the bloodiest century in history were men and women of great humanity and prophetic courage who peopled Pedro's world. In India was Gandhi. In the United States, Martin Luther King Jr. and his wife, Loretta, and also Dorothy Day and Thomas Merton. In Europe was the philosopher, mystic, and political activist Simone Weil, and the heroes opposing the Nazi regime, such as Etty Hillesum, Dietrich Bonhoeffer, and the Carmelite nun Edith Stein. The insights of Teilhard de Chardin and Karl Rahner began to emerge. In El Salvador, the Jesuit priest Rutilio Grande was murdered, and Óscar Romero was assassinated for his defense of the poor in 1980. The list goes on and on.

Massive changes, too long delayed, rocked the Catholic Church. Inspired by the Spirit, Pope John XXIII convoked the Second Vatican Council from 1962 to 1965. It ushered in a process known as *aggiornamento*, or updating, that brought freedom and life to the Christian community and illuminated the Christian mission in relation to the world. It ignited a process of change and renewal in response to the signs of the times: liturgy, devotions, and religious life were all updated. The Church began to understand its congregation not as a passive flock but as the pilgrim people of God.

The universal call to holiness was affirmed: relationships were deepened with the other great religions and Churches; ecumenism became acceptable; freedom of conscience and the rights of error were acknowledged. The council's final document proclaimed in its opening sentence a new solidarity with the human family, which was music to Jesuit ears: "The joys and hopes, the grief and anguish of the people of our time, are the joys and hopes, the grief and anguish of the followers of Christ as well."[36]

Pedro, then, played his part in a century rich with giants who gave their lives for justice and thinkers who fostered a peak of Catholic idealism.

## Family

Pedro was born on November 14, 1907, in Bilbao, in northern Spain, a city of more than eighty-two thousand inhabitants. His home and the cathedral in which he was baptized are still extant. Like Ignatius, he was Basque. While World War I was brewing in Europe, Gandhi's passive resistance campaign was getting under way in South Africa, and Lenin was founding the Russian Communist Party (the Bolsheviks), back in Spain the Arrupe family was a happy and comfortable one.

Pedro, the youngest, had four sisters, so he was always treated with great affection and loved his family deeply in return. This helps us understand that joyous, optimistic, and loving personality that was to be so tested later. His father, Marcelino, was an architect and a businessman: the steel industry was strong in Bilbao at the time. He also edited the local paper, which may have helped his son to write as copiously and incisively as he did. Marcelino had a magnificent tenor voice, which Pedro inherited and used later to entertain his Jesuit brethren. His mother, Dolores, used to say that her son would be a priest, to which young Pedro would nonchalantly respond, "Mom says I will be a priest; well, I will be a priest." Sadly, she died when he was only nine, leaving an enduring gap in the family; his father passed away when Pedro was twenty.

Pedro's parents had seen to it that he got the best available Catholic education. He lived in a Catholic atmosphere, and there are no indications that he ever experienced doubts regarding his faith. Joining the Congregation of Mary Immaculate and St. Stanislaus Kostka brought him into contact with the Jesuits. At age seven, he attended the nearby school of the Piarist fathers and was known as a happy, open, and bright student. He loved theater, music, and opera. Sensitive, idealistic, and charming, he was captivated by the desire to heal people, so at sixteen, as Spain became a dictatorship, he went to live with his sister Margarita in the great city of Madrid, where he studied medicine. Those whose courses he attended declared that a brilliant career awaited him.

## Meeting Poverty in Madrid

Having moved to a student residence, Pedro and some friends joined the Society of St. Vincent de Paul. Visiting the slums, he tells us, opened a totally new and disturbing world to him. There he encountered the misery and abandonment of widows, sick people begging for alms, starving children. He recalled a little boy munching on a yam. "What are you doing?" Pedro asked.

"Having breakfast."

"But it's four o'clock!"

"I know, but this is the first food I've had today."

"You haven't had any food all day? Doesn't your father work?"

"We hardly ever have any food. We never eat more than once a day, and my father doesn't work because I don't have one."[37]

One shock was followed by others. He tells us that with a companion he knocked on a door in a large house and went in, where they were received with profound silence. Six disheveled and half-naked children took refuge in their mothers' skirts. The furniture in sight was a large bed with a shabby blanket, and little else. One of the women, with a heroic sense of humor, asked: "How do you like our palace? Here, where you see us, we eat and sleep. Here the kids play and we work. On the rainy days when they can't go out, they give us headaches with their screaming. You must have heard the noise when you were outside."

"And where do you all sleep?" Pedro asked.

"In the bed."

"All eight of you?"

"Yes, all eight. We'll show you! Now everybody, get into bed, each one in place. Let these gentlemen see how you sleep."

Like a flock of birds, the little ones went running to their nest and stretched out on the frayed blanket. The woman continued: "What do you think? Half a football team in the sack! We women have a hard time sleeping there because our bodies sink down and the kids tumble on us; but they're our children, so we forgive them everything."

Stunned, the young men were silent. Then the woman spoke again: "The bed's the least of our worries, because the kids at least get their sleep. On cold days we have them stay in bed all day, covered with the blanket, but it's difficult. What's worse is the matter of food: we have no pension or women's aid. The only income is from our work, and one of us has to mind the kids while the other works."

"What do the little ones eat?" the visitors asked.

"Almost nothing, really. In the morning, some soup and whatever bread can be found. In the middle of the day, beans and bread."

As they departed, Pedro and his companion gave out candy and some alms to cheers from the children.[38]

Such were Pedro's first encounters with the structural injustices of the world, and they left an indelible emotional seal on his soul. Similar experiences sprinkled his later life and nurtured his passionate concern for those at the bottom of society. Care for the poor—the preferential option for the poor—became his concern: for him, truly human living, he felt, must be a total gift to others, especially to those most at risk, those whom no one else was serving. Where the poor are, God is, because the poor are the friends of God.

Throughout his life he loved the poor and they, him. Just one example: In the 1970s, after Pedro celebrated Mass in a Latin American slum, a burly man in the congregation said to him:

"Come with me and I will share something precious with you." It was the evening of a long day. They walked a distance, climbed a hill, and came to the poor man's house. Then his host said: "Sit here and see the sunset, how beautiful it is." They watched it in silence and awe: then the man said: "Señor, I did not know how to thank you for all that you have done for us. I have nothing to give you, but

I thought you would like to see this sunset. It pleased you, didn't it? *Buona sera!*"[39]

It was his gift to Pedro, who saw that the poor have so much to give and that life is not only about doing things for other people but also, as here, about being in solidarity with them, sharing in their sense of the mystery and beauty of creation.

## "What Am I Doing Here?"

Pedro continued his undergraduate studies in Madrid: he studied hard but also enjoyed theater, music, and opera. He continued to visit the impoverished, helped his fellow students with their courses, and won a major academic prize at the end of his third year. His father's death while Pedro was in Madrid devastated him and the close-knit family at home. Mostly, a radical question had begun to niggle at him: "What am I doing here?"

I began to ask myself more frequently: Why have I come into the world? To live a few years of sterile anonymity and then face the other life without having done anything worthwhile? I put the blame on those six street urchins in their poverty and their tenement, because they made me think; they first alerted me to the fact that I was drifting. This was a great gift of God.[40]

# Cures in Lourdes

At the beginning of the academic year of 1926, Pedro did not reappear in class. He had spent the month of July with his family in Lourdes: "I arrived at Lourdes with much curiosity. I didn't know what I would find there: there was a kind of presentiment that I myself didn't know how to define." Despite not having completed his medical studies, he obtained a certificate that allowed him to assist in the Bureau for the Verification of Miracles, and he had the good fortune to witness what appeared to be three miracles. What follows is an abbreviated version of his own account.

The first miracle was that of a young nun who found herself in a humanly hopeless state. She had Pott's disease, a type of tuberculosis that affects the backbone: several of her vertebrae were already eaten away. Half of her body had long been imprisoned in a plaster cast, and she was totally immobilized by paralysis. But she uttered no complaints, smiled affectionately, and tried to pass a few words from her unmoving lips. As the Blessed Sacrament was moving along, Jesus Christ and the paralyzed nun found themselves face-to-face: a loving contact took place between them, something instantaneous. Crying out, the nun sat up on her stretcher, reached out her arms toward the Eucharist, and fell forward on her knees.

"I am cured!" was all she could say. And the whole crowd shouted in response: "Miracle!"

The second miracle was that of a seventy-five-year-old woman from Brussels. She suffered from terrible stomach cancer and was beyond medical help. She reasoned: "If I go to Lourdes, the Virgin can cure me, if that is what is good for me." Despite all objections she traveled across France and arrived in Lourdes more dead than alive. She was taken to bathe in the waters, and back at the hospital, she began to eat her food. Within three days she was walking around in perfect health: X-rays showed no trace of the cancer.

The third case was that of a young man whose body had been twisted and contorted by polio. His mother was reciting the rosary in a loud voice and from time to time would sigh, "*María santíssima*, help us." The moment came when the bishop was to bless the young man, who looked at the host with the same faith with which the paralytic in the Gospels must have looked at Jesus. After the bishop had made the sign of the cross with the Blessed Sacrament, the young man rose from his stretcher, and the crowd, filled with joy, cried out: "Miracle! Miracle!" Again, Pedro, with his medical certificate and position at the bureau, was able to examine him:

> I felt God so close to me in his miracles that he dragged me violently behind him. And I saw him so close to those who suffer, those who weep, and those whose lives are shattered. An ardent desire burned within me to imitate

him in the same closeness to the world's human debris, to those despised by a society that doesn't even suspect that there are souls pulsating beneath such great sorrow.[41]

# Vocation

Whence Arrupe's vocation? He tells us:

> I had been an eyewitness of a true miracle worked by Jesus Christ in the Eucharist! I was filled with an immense joy: I sensed God very close and tugging at me. I seemed to be standing by the side of Jesus, and as I sensed his almighty power the world around me began to appear extremely small.[42]

Three months later, in January 1927, he entered the novitiate of the Society of Jesus in Loyola, Spain. He was not yet twenty: the medical fraternity was dismayed; his family, devastated. It was a sign of his "normality" that nobody had expected this turn in his life. He told them: "It is something bigger than me." One of his sisters told him boldly: "Go, Pedro, if you see it clearly. Without a doubt it is a grace that has been obtained by Dad's death."[43] "If you see it clearly," his sister had said. Pedro often seemed to see clearly.

Early in his formation, Pedro asked to be sent to Japan, where Francis Xavier had labored almost four centuries before. But he was told to wait, and wait he did, for ten years.

Asked why he wanted to go to Japan, he responded that his only missionary motive was God's will:

> During my annual retreat in 1929—less than two years after joining the Jesuits—I had a clear vision that my vocation was to be a missionary and that it would lead me to Japan. And don't ask me what "vision" means: it's a question of an intimate experience that no word can describe and that can be understood only as it unfolds in time.[44]

## The Closeness of God

Pedro's sense of God's closeness was engraved in his soul and is critically important to our understanding of what went on in him and sustained him throughout his long life: this sense stayed with him in his joys and sorrows, his achievements and failures. He would have made his own the insight of Teilhard de Chardin SJ, his contemporary and one of his favorite authors:

> By means of all created things, without exception, the divine assails us, penetrates and moulds us. We imagined it as distant and inaccessible, when in fact we live steeped in its burning layers.[45]

From a monastic vantage point, Thomas Merton came to the same awareness:

Every moment and every event of every man's life on earth plants something in his soul. For just as the wind carries thousands of winged seeds so each moment brings with it germs of spiritual vitality that come to rest imperceptibly in the minds and wills of men. Most of these unnumbered seeds perish and are lost, because men are not prepared to receive them: for such seeds as these cannot spring up anywhere except in the good soil of freedom, spontaneity, and love.[46]

Every moment, every event—awareness of God as active in every detail of life is life changing, disconcerting, and sometimes uncomfortable. How many of us have the sensitivity to be able to say, as Pedro did, "All has unfolded according to the will of God"? He elaborated later on this assertion: "The radical turning points in my life's paths have always been unexpected. But sooner or later I have had to recognize the hand of God that gave the helm a bold twist."[47]

After the difficult passage between Pope Paul VI and himself in 1975, mediated by Cardinal Benelli, Arrupe confided that he was expecting to be dismissed by the pope. He is said to have added: "I don't think he'll do it, but if he does I will need only five minutes to get my things together and return to Japan."[48]

# Jesuit Formation, 1927–1938

Jesuit formation used to last about fourteen years: ordination to priesthood, it was quipped, was the reward of a well-spent life. Some said that Jesuit formation took so long because of the candidates' stupidity! The novice Pedro Arrupe would have become deeply immersed in Ignatius's story and learned about the Society and his own suitability for it. Various experiences aided this process, such as manual labor, an extended pilgrimage undertaken in poverty, and apostolic work tailored to his capacity. The experience of the monthlong Spiritual Exercises, central to the Jesuit spirit, facilitated Pedro's falling in love ever more deeply with the Jesus of the Gospels.

The two years of his novitiate were a time of solid growth in companionship with his fellow novices, in prayer, and in knowledge of his strengths and limitations. Most importantly, he was helped to discern whether God was calling him to the Jesuit way of life. When that was settled, he was then allowed to take perpetual vows of poverty, chastity, and obedience.

Two years of studies in the humanities followed at Loyola in Spain, and in 1931 he began his philosophy studies at Oña, Burgos, also in Spain. It was there that he had intense experiences of God. In one of these he seemed to "see everything as new," a phrase that Ignatius had used to hint at his own transforming experience near the Cardoner River in 1522. But in 1932 the Jesuit order was expelled from Spain by the government, which perceived it to be closely aligned to the wealthy and powerful of Spanish society. All Jesuit property was seized, and 2,700 Spanish Jesuits sought refuge elsewhere in Europe. This was a shattering experience of disruption, and it raised for Pedro questions about the secular world's perception of the Church, an issue that would shape his future thinking.

He and his fellow students found a home in Marneffe, Belgium, where they could continue their philosophy program. Because of his pre-novitiate studies, Pedro skipped the formation period known as regency, where he would have taught in a Jesuit school. In 1933 he began his study of theology with the German Jesuits at the Ignatiuskolleg in Valkenburg, Holland, and was ordained on July 30, 1936, in Marneffe. In 1936 and 1937 he completed his fourth year of theology at St. Mary's College, in the state of Kansas, and because of his ability and earlier medical background, he and his work were earmarked for doctoral studies in bioethics.

## Tridentine Theology

As a student, Arrupe would have worked obediently through the textbook theology of the day, with lectures in Latin, but later in life he enjoyed Karl Rahner, Henri de Lubac, and

Teilhard de Chardin, all of whom were suspect in Roman circles before Vatican II. Over the lecture halls lay the dark shadow of modernism, "the compendium of all heresies," condemned in 1907 by Pope Pius X. Teachers of theology had to take an oath against it by stating that Christian truth is absolute, immutable, and not subject to new interpretation. Modern ideas and groundbreaking scholarship were viewed with suspicion. Teilhard de Chardin had been exiled to China in 1926 and forbidden to teach or to publish his findings on the unfolding of the cosmos, the evolution of humankind, and the full realization of creation in Christ. The oath against modernism remained officially in place until rescinded by Pope Paul VI in 1967.

An anonymous commentator remarks of this time:

> Although sometimes, to the despair of his advisors, Arrupe's theological categories and vocabulary are those of Tridentine Catholicism, the central thrust of his thinking in many respects anticipated the Second Vatican Council. Taking kindly the counsel of the years, he has gracefully surrendered some of the hard and fast dogmatism of the tradition in which he was reared. He himself has a strongly hierarchic, even monarchical, view of the Church, together with an immense personal reverence for the pope. He frequently speaks as if the Church were identical with the hierarchy. But he can understand and accept that many Jesuits today cannot see the Church in such simple terms.[49]

In 1937 Pedro went to Cleveland, Ohio, for his tertianship, a reflective year of spiritual renewal that Jesuits undertake after completing their studies and before pronouncing final vows. He made the full Spiritual Exercises for the second time and studied in depth the Jesuit *Constitutions* and other writings of Ignatius. His pastoral gifts found expression in the local prisons, where he served Spanish-speaking immigrants. He had a way with the prisoners because of his simplicity, honesty, and compassion, and he won high commendation for his gentle approach.

His deep devotion and his desire for greater service seem to have led him to take—with permission—a vow of perfection. "The mirror of the soul has to be always perfectly clear, without the slightest misting over. Hence now, if ever, the vow of perfection takes on a special relevance."[50] He explains in his commentary on the Exercises, written in Japan:

Sanctity is attained not by difficult means but by always seeking God's will . . . This is the surest way to reach the state of "being perfect as your heavenly Father is perfect" . . . Constantly seeking God's will, instead of causing us anxiety, will always bring us great peace . . . It does not mean that a person has to be constantly examining himself and continually stirring up his fervor. That would make life impossible and therefore would never be God's will.[51]

# 4

## JAPAN, 1938–1965

## A Dream Fulfilled

Arrupe was finally missioned to Japan in 1938, while the senseless horrors of the Spanish Civil War were still multiplying and Pope Pius XI was warning of the immediate threat of another war in Europe. Arrupe sailed from Seattle and arrived in Yokohama two weeks later. Because he spent twenty-seven years in Japan—more than a third of his active life—I share here a sketch of that land and its people, whom he came to know and love.

An Irish Jesuit, Gerard J. Bourke, who was missioned there in 1951, fourteen years after Arrupe arrived, wrote the following in an early letter home:

Sometimes I wonder if it is all a colossal dream—this "strange new world that has such people in it." The teeming population, the packed trains and buses, the thousands of small wooden houses packed tightly together, the gaily coloured streets, the wooden clogs and colourful kimonos, the kind and courteous older folk, the friendly and lovable children, the Buddhist temples and Shinto shrines where strange celebrations are held on occasions, and stately Mt Fuji rearing its snow-capped peak into the clouds, reminding the thoughtful of a world beyond—all these create an atmosphere which it is impossible to convey in a letter.[52]

# History of Japan

The necklace of islands known as Japan lies at the edge of the Pacific Ocean, beyond the shores of Korea and China. A land of earthquakes and tsunamis, Japan was settled by migrants from China and Korea before the Christian era. Slowly, its many kingdoms and tribes became unified under a centralized government, nominally controlled by an imperial dynasty that has continued to modern times, albeit in a ceremonial role.

Although not practiced as a religion, Confucianism deeply influenced the Japanese way of life. Confucius, born in China in 551 BCE, proposed the practice of proper forms of conduct, especially in social and familial relationships. A strict class system developed, and Japan's contacts with the outside world were few. Buddhism came a thousand years later from India via China and promoted the concept of the fully enlightened human being. Shintoism, indigenous to Japan, holds the belief that all things, animate and inanimate, possess a spirit. Today, the Japanese visit both Shinto shrines and Buddhist temples.

Over the centuries, external conflicts were frequent, mainly with China and Korea. In 1543 the Portuguese became the first Europeans to reach Japan, and they had a significant impact, not least by introducing firearms to Japanese warfare. In 1549 the Jesuit Francis Xavier and three companions arrived: they were welcomed for a brief period, but conversion was forbidden. To the Japanese mind, the concept of a god who created everything, including evil, could not be good, and the notion of eternal punishment distressed a people who strongly venerated their ancestors. In 1597 twenty-six native Christians were martyred in Nagasaki, and an edict of 1635 forbade the practice of Christianity under pain of death. A long period of isolation followed.

The American Perry Expedition, of 1853 and 1854, forced Japan to open up to foreign trade, and a new national leadership transformed the nation into a Western-style empire. Japan became a major political player in the Far East, and its invasion of Manchuria in 1931 escalated into a prolonged war with China. Such was the Japan into which the novice missioner Pedro Arrupe arrived in 1938.

During World War II, on December 7, 1941, Japan's attack on Pearl Harbor led to war with the United States. Japan's forces soon became overextended but held out in spite of Allied air attacks. Emperor Hirohito finally announced Japan's surrender on August 15, 1945, following the Soviet invasion of Manchuria, and the Allied powers enacted a new constitution in 1947 that transformed Japan into a constitutional monarchy. Japan joined the United Nations in 1956 and soon became a world economic power.

This was the background against which Pedro worked in Japan from 1938 until he was called to Rome in 1965 to become the twenty-eighth general of the Jesuits. Despite strenuous pastoral work by the Jesuits and other missionaries in Japan, there are currently only 500,000 Catholics there, in a population of more than 120 million.

## Culture

At the age of thirty-one, Pedro immediately began to study Japanese in Nagatsuka, near Hiroshima, and over the years he achieved fluency. He spoke six other languages as well: English, French, German, Italian, Latin, and Spanish. He could also speak a touch of Basque—but someone commented that he actually spoke Spanish in seven languages! Mastery of the language was one of the toughest tests for a European trying to enter fully into Japanese culture. Before the sixth century CE, the Japanese had no written language; they then began to use Chinese characters or ideograms. The characters have two pronunciations, one purely Japanese, the other sounding like the Chinese symbol. Hence the complexity! Each character may have as many as thirty strokes and up to seven meanings.

But more than grappling with a mix of unknown sounds and symbols, immersion in Japanese culture demanded a whole new way of life. Pedro arrived with no preparation for a history and culture built on foundations totally different from his own. His early months were spent learning to practice Japanese customs: smiling, bowing his head, removing his shoes when entering a house. He slowly learned the language, enlivening it innocently with a mix of Spanish, Basque, and English. Remarkably, he finally reached a level of proficiency that enabled him to translate into Japanese and write commentaries on Ignatius's *Spiritual Exercises* and some of the works of St. John of the Cross. Happily, he soon discovered that more important than what he said was what and who he really was.

When living in Yamaguchi, Pedro discovered what seemed a strange friendliness among the people: "All the inhabitants contributed something impalpable out of their own spiritual refinement." His love of music helped him, and he once played his fiddle in a Yamaguchi square to gather an audience, much as Xavier had rung his bell four hundred years earlier. We don't know whether either initiative was an apostolic triumph! But at a public celebration of St. Francis Xavier, who had visited the city during the sixteenth century, the opening speaker, a history professor at Yamaguchi University, took a decidedly non-Catholic approach to the saint:

> Xavier's heart beat strong with the spirit of adventure and an intrepid heroism. But he came with the cross in one hand and a sword in the other, hiding a suit of armour under a plain missionary cassock. He came with the banner of faith to prepare for the occupation of our country, to undermine our nation.[53]

Pedro immediately sensed an ancient ancestral pride that considered itself invincible and led to foreigners being viewed with suspicion. Without knowing what line to take, he had to respond: "I presented Xavier as the saint whose only goal was to bring happiness to the Japanese people . . . There were moments when I thought that Xavier himself was speaking through my mouth as he had spoken four centuries before in that same place." To offset the charge that Xavier was always on the move he remarked that, if he was a restless saint, it was because the Holy Spirit never nods off![54]

## Character

Impressed by the way young people could sit for hours on their mats in the lotus posture, Pedro came to see that he must wait patiently for them to communicate what they really wanted to say. He discovered that God was there before him. Working in a settlement barracks, he found a young catechumen spending hours in prayer, without moving, totally concentrated on the tabernacle.

"What are you doing?" he asked.

"Nothing."

"What do you mean, nothing?"

"Well, I am just here."

To Pedro, she was combining her "being here" of Zen and the "being here" of Christian contemplation.[55]

Likewise, he came upon his housekeeper praying before a statue of the Buddha that her deceased husband had given her. She had become a devout Catholic, but she was praying to her husband's God. Then there were the two poor children in catechism class who had placed their presents for Jesus in a cardboard box. One added the note: "For your sake, Jesus, I have made peace with Takeo-san, even though he was the one to blame and I wasn't. To console him I will take him home as if nothing had happened."[56]

Pedro attributed his pastoral successes to the fact that he shared with those who wished his devotion to the Sacred

Heart of Jesus. Early on in Japan, he gathered the Spanish missionaries who consecrated their labors to the Sacred Heart of Jesus. He commented afterward:

> God heard us . . . but wished his loving and redeeming Providence to be accompanied by our disillusionment, by our love and by our tears. He wished to test our faith, as he did with Peter when he walked on the water . . . The external reply to our dedication was prison for me . . . but today we can speak of Christ without external interference or unfounded suspicions."[57]

This was the secret of his energy as he began his pastoral life. He came across as someone deeply in love, and he was indeed in love with the person of Christ. He believed that the effectiveness of his ministry depended not on him, but on the Lord, and wherever he went, he tried to leave the memory of the heart of Jesus Christ behind him.[58]

## "You Do Not Lie!"

Convinced of the importance of enculturation, Pedro studied and practiced Zen meditation and is often portrayed in a meditative Zen posture. Zen originated in India in the sixth century, was then brought to China, and began to flourish in Japan from the twelfth century as a mode of gaining insight into the mystery of one's deeper self. The tea ceremony, the art of archery, and the beautiful rock gardens are all designed to facilitate this encounter. For example, the stylized Zen garden imitates the essence of a natural landscape, enabling the meditator to grasp the true meaning of life as distinct from what it appears to be. Arrupe's own efforts at enculturation spoke of humility and respect, of a reverence for the prior presence of the Spirit in the culture to which he was bringing the gospel. He noted that in Japan the image of the Good Shepherd is not usable, since there are neither flocks nor sheep. The same is true for the lily, which for Christians is a symbol of purity. So he set himself to learn the philosophy behind Japanese practices such as the tea ceremony, archery, and flower arrangement.[59]

Pedro found that the Japanese judged a person's interior spirit by observing external behavior. When he was offering Mass, his authenticity, inner harmony, simplicity, and transparency of soul likely did more to convince than any words or activities. He tells of an experience catechizing adults. An old man watched him intensely but for six months said not a word either for or against Pedro's message. Puzzled, Pedro finally dared to ask, "What do you think of my explanations?" The man replied: "I cannot give an opinion because I have heard nothing. I am completely deaf. However, for me it is sufficient just to look into your eyes. You do not lie. What you believe, I believe also."[60]

## Solitary Confinement

Three years passed before the Japanese attack on Pearl Harbor in December 1941 and America's entry into World War II. Pedro was arrested on charges of espionage and spent thirty-three days in solitary confinement. Deprived of the Eucharist and of all human comfort, he says:

> I experienced deep pain for the lack of the Eucharist, but there was at the same time a feeling of the faithful and consoling presence of our Lord. What loneliness there was: I then appreciated what the Eucharist means to a priest, to a Jesuit, for whom the Mass and the tabernacle are the very centre of his life. I believe that this was the month that I learned the most in all my life.[61]

He had time to contemplate the possibility of tortures such as many of his brethren had endured before him. These are graphically depicted in Martin Scorsese's 2016 film *Silence*, based on the novel of the same name by Shusaku Endo. He prayed for courage and found God close: "It was beautiful, the solitude with Christ, a mystical experience, nothing in my cell, only me and Christ." His eyes would fill with tears in telling this story. As with his expulsion from Spain in 1932, he had a direct experience of personal injustice because he, a Spaniard, had offered his life simply to bring the Good News to the people of Japan. He began to ponder how the message of Christ could ever be heard above the din of hatred and violence.

Interrogated for an unbroken thirty-six hours, he found himself astonished that the Spirit of wisdom prompted his replies, as promised by Jesus to his disciples (Mark 13:11). Again there is that sense of divine closeness in Pedro, even in the depths of pain and misery. On Christmas night his spirits sank low: it seemed rather to be Good Friday! Then he began to hear a soft murmur outside his cell and wondered what it might mean. Had his execution squad arrived?

> There arose a soft, sweet, consoling Christmas carol, one which I myself had taught my Christians. I burst into tears. Heedless of the danger of being themselves imprisoned, they had come to console me. It lasted for a few minutes, and then there was silence again: they had gone, and I was left to myself. But I felt that Jesus had descended into my heart, and that night I made the best spiritual communion of my life.[62]

## Director of Novices

When freed from prison, Pedro was assigned to the formation of Japanese novices in 1942 and named rector of the novitiate (located at Nagatsuka, not far from Hiroshima) and superior of the local district of Yamaguchi. His twelve years of forming novices gave him a deep appreciation of the mind and heart of Ignatius and of the challenges involved in winning over the human heart to humble and unconditional service to God.

Slowly he learned that the most effective way into the soul of the Japanese was through profound person-to-person relationship. The Japanese people's curiosity about the mysteries of Christian faith did not necessarily result in conversion. They would attend Mass but then return to their mysterious inner world. Working with the novices, he found that they were patient but at the same time impenetrable. It was necessary, he said, to undo their concept of "god" to lead them to a greater God. When they discovered this Being, they felt great amazement: decisiveness and integrity characterized them when they became convinced.

He had no qualms about challenging these would-be Jesuits on whom the future of the mission in Japan would depend:

> Stay at home if this idea makes you unsettled or nervous. Do not come to us if you love the Church like a stepmother. Do not come to us if you think that in so doing you will be doing the Society of Jesus a favour.
>
> Come, if serving Christ is at the centre of your life. Come, if you have an open spirit, a reasonably open mind, and a heart larger than the world. Come, if you know how to tell a joke and can laugh with others. And on occasions you should be willing to laugh at yourself![63]

# The Oven of Hiroshima

The young Jesuits in Japan were starving in wartime conditions as they prepared to serve the spiritual needs of the Japanese people. Meanwhile in the United States, the Manhattan Project—the creation of the atomic bomb—was under way in top secrecy and at immense cost.

On the Feast of the Transfiguration, August 6, 1945, the chaplain's prayer for the success of the flight and crew of the *Enola Gay*—the plane carrying the bomb—was read at the military airport at Tinian:

> Lord God, hear the prayer of those who love you. We ask you to be with those who are going to battle our enemies. Keep them and protect them, we ask you, so that they may fly safely to their objective. May they, as we ourselves, know your force and your power; may our men, with your arms, succeed in bringing this war to an end, so that we can once again experience peace on earth.[64]

While homilies for the Catholic feast day carried a message of hope for humanity's future and spoke of divine fire descending from heaven to renew the face of the earth, the A-bomb was dropped on the unsuspecting city of Hiroshima. It fell to earth with a blinding flash, a crashing thunder, a devastating blast, and a deceptively beautiful mushroom cloud, and it changed the history of humankind. High over the skies of Hiroshima, the pilot, Colonel Paul Tibbett, looked down from the cockpit and, seeing what remained of the city, exclaimed in horror: "My God, what have we done?"

Returning home by ship from a meeting with the Soviet Union, President Harry Truman received a telegram: "Results clear cut successful in all respects." Truman shouted out gleefully to the sailors: "Guys, we have sent them a twenty-thousand-ton block of TNT!" The sailors cheered with delight.[65]

On that fateful day Pedro was living on the outskirts of Hiroshima in the town of Nagatsuka. He wrote a dramatic account of what had happened at 8:15 on that dreadful morning.[66]

> There was a blinding flash, a huge explosion, and then doors, windows, and walls fell on the Jesuit community in smithereens. No one was injured. Not knowing what had happened, they climbed a hill and saw below the ruins of Hiroshima.
>
> Since the houses were made of wood, paper, and straw, and it was at a time when the first meal of the day was being prepared in all the kitchens, the flames contacting the electric current turned the entire city into one enormous lake of fire.[67]

Pedro and his companions felt helpless: they had been spared the blast by a small hill that stood between them and the devastated city. They knelt and prayed, then Pedro decided to make their house into a field hospital. Torrents of rain helped dampen the fires, and after twelve hours they were able to enter the destroyed city. They squeezed 150 wounded people into their small house, and, using his medical skills, Pedro triaged the patients into various groups. Many had been burned by flames; others developed huge blisters; some had their clothes melted into their bodies. No one at that moment knew what caused the wounds; only later they were recognized as the aftereffects of infrared radiation.

Two hundred children perished in one school when its roof collapsed; hundreds of others were left searching for their parents. The limbs of many people were calcified. A person sitting on a flight of stone steps outside a bank was instantly incinerated: the surface of the steps turned white, and that person reduced to a shadow on the stone. Many of the wounded fled to the river to escape burning, but when the tide came in, they were buried in mud and died by drowning.

## The Medic

Pedro used his office desk as an operating table. The suffering of victims he saw was frightful, but they uttered not a word of complaint. A young married man whose whole body seemed to be a running sore kept repeating, "Father, don't hesitate to hurt me; I can take it, but just save me." He and his faithful wife stayed on for eight months and were finally able to resume their lives. Some parents found their children alive and living with the Jesuits and threw themselves at their feet in wordless gratitude.

Pedro had led the first rescue party into the doomed city. He brought home scarred humans who had been burned, boiled, skinned, deafened, and blinded, but they were survivors of what only later was recognized as an atomic bomb: a new word had entered the world's vocabulary. He said later: "We were in effect the first guinea pigs in this experimentation." The little band of Jesuit helpers had been warned by the authorities: "Do not enter the city: there is a gas in the air that will kill people for the next seventy years." But they went in anyway and helped to cremate 50,000 bodies and to care for at least a few of the 120,000 wounded.

Pedro often spoke about the Hiroshima experience when traveling the world in search of personnel and funding for the Japanese mission. For him the bomb was "a mystery of iniquity, a permanent experience outside of history, engraved on my memory." He saw the event as a moment when time stopped, like the clock on the wall, frozen at 8:15. It was, he said, an ongoing moment of eternity. It also gave him an immense and enduring energy to do all that was humanly possible to build a better world.

# Where Is God?

Questioning again arose in Pedro's mind: Where is God in all this, and what should be the role of the Catholic Church and the Jesuits in the face of such horrors?

Ignatius had been graced with great clarity about his way forward during his Cardoner River experience in 1522: throughout his life he kept returning to it when searching for the next step to take. For Pedro the dropping of the atomic bomb on the innocents of Hiroshima was a parallel defining moment to which he often returned. The event laid bare the chasm between good and evil, between God's project for humankind and humans' distortion of it. Humanity, he said, is trapped in a net of steel, out of which it is difficult to break.[68] He was left with a total abhorrence of violence, later shown in his critique of those who took up arms to resist unjust regimes. Were he to be canonized, Pedro might well be named the patron saint of nuclear nonviolence!

If we ask what made Pedro respond as he did, an Ignatian theme suggests the answer. In his Spiritual Exercises (No. 53), Ignatius has the retreatant question the crucified Lord: "What ought I do?" Whenever a need emerges, God may want help. So it was for Pedro that fateful day: instead of standing apart and celebrating spiritually the Transfiguration of Jesus, he felt inwardly called to go into the ravaged city to help those whose lives had been destroyed.

# Provincial Superior

Pedro remained as novice director until 1954, when he was appointed vice-provincial. It was a challenging task to continue the work of evangelization in a nation broken in spirit. He maintained his sense of humor, and when examining the construction of a college that looked like a bunker, he asked with a smile, "How's the flour factory going?"[69] His commitment was never in doubt either. Toward the close of his active life, he remarked when encouraging his brethren working in Thailand:

> You see little success externally in a country that is mostly Buddhist and where there are so few Catholics. I think I can speak from experience! In Japan you may find a parish priest baptizing only two people in ten years. What is in question here is not external success but commitment.[70]

In 1958 Japan became a full Jesuit province, and Arrupe was named provincial, a post he held until the fateful 1965 Jesuit gathering in Rome at which he was elected superior general. Unknowingly, he was being prepared for the task: an indomitable traveler, he circled the globe several times, seeking personnel and finance for the mission in Japan, and so came to a unique experiential knowledge of the world and the Society. He had, as was said, a universal passport! Under his guidance the province reached a membership of three hundred Jesuits from some thirty countries, which meant that he had the task of coordinating a group of strong-minded men from different backgrounds and national and cultural outlooks. He managed to hold them together through the bonds of the Spiritual Exercises, the *Constitutions*, and the commitment to Christ's mission through obedience.

# 5

---

# SUPERIOR GENERAL,
# 1965–1983

On May 22, 1965, I had the task of reading to the Jesuit community in Galway Pedro Arrupe's acceptance speech on his election as superior general. Those who had been studying the candidates had considered him a likely choice, and he was elected on the third ballot. He was fifty-eight and a Basque, and he was coming from Japan, with its aura of mystery and its tragic history. It was a moment of high emotion for us: our lives would be in his hands, and we asked ourselves what we might expect from him and he from us.

# Gifts and Limits

Arrupe had come to Rome as an outsider with a return ticket, a humble missionary from the other end of the earth. In the discussions preparatory to the election, he had tried only to convince his brethren that the Society of Jesus must adapt radically to meet the needs of the contemporary world. His listeners had been impressed: many already knew him from his travels on behalf of the mission in Japan. On the positive side were his age and health, his boundless zeal, his insight into enculturation, his capacity to effect change, and his gift for communication and animation. He was seen to have a special gift for easy and trusting relationships and was a natural leader. Because of his travels he had also developed an excellent knowledge of the state of the Society and could manage communicating in many languages. He had been tried in the inferno of Hiroshima and not found wanting: he would have the courage to lead the Society on new paths, and by discerning the signs of the times, adapt it to ever-changing circumstances. Those who had become close to him knew of his Christ-centered view of the world and how deeply God was the absolute for him. Pedro loved God's world, had a special concern for the poor, and was willing to rethink everything in the light of the gospel. He was also fully at home in Ignatian spirituality.

On the negative side one might have mentioned excessive idealism, a naïveté shown in trusting too easily, a poor record of overall strategy and organization, and an inability to impose discipline. Another drawback included his ignorance of Vatican diplomacy, given that he had never studied in Rome or spent significant time there.

## The One Who Gives Me Strength

Arrupe began his speech of acceptance by quoting from Jeremiah about being unable to speak. He says elsewhere:

> I had no qualifications, and I found myself facing the Society, its great scholars, its great doctors, its great spiritual masters. Here was a little man who had parachuted in: what could he do? It was a moment of great confusion for me.[71]

His speech to the delegates continued:

> These words of Jeremiah express my feeling of smallness. It is however evident that God's will has done this. "Do not be afraid, for I am with you." I have never felt before so intimately our Lord's word: "Cut off from me, you can do nothing." Still, since the choice came from God, I can yet say in humility with St. Paul: "There is nothing I cannot master with the help of the One who gives me strength."[72]

He was articulate, incisive, comprehensive, intelligible, and authentic, and he soon became the darling of the media. Most Jesuits experienced his presence as the incarnation of goodwill and encouragement. He was himself transparent through and through, with no hidden agendas: one never had to wonder what he was really thinking. He had the gift of commending tough ideals in a persuasive way; all he asked for in his audiences was a spirit of openness and generosity. His radiant smile invited a positive response. His logic was persuasive:

> To be a companion of Jesus . . . is to love Jesus Christ with all one's soul . . . Jesus Christ does not want half-hearted people among his companions ("friends in the Lord"). From that follows everything else: this companion . . . is a person who, through love of Christ, is totally committed, under the standard of the cross, in the decisive struggle of our times for the faith and for the justice which that faith itself demands.[73]

He knew he would be bound to suffer as superior general, and he solemnly warned that the mission of the Society would surely bring Jesuits face-to-face with the violence of the Passion. But in all this he radiated a joyful honesty and simplicity. He had a big smile for everyone, and it came from his heart: he loved his brethren.

# Need for Jesuit Renewal

Arrupe's *Retreat Notes*, written just for himself within three months of his election, show that he was keenly aware of the Society's need for deep renewal. We will explore these notes further below; here, we focus on Pedro's first thoughts as superior general on Jesuit renewal. The Society, he writes, needs to be "toned up" as a muscle in preparation for exertion, or tuned up as a musical instrument before being played. Inspired by the daring of the Japanese kamikaze squadrons, he ponders the formation of similar squads, and in fact he used this image, in a positive way, on at least one public occasion in reference to the possibility of squads of men dedicated to intense spirituality, poverty, and abnegation. (It helps to know that in Japanese *kamikaze* means "the divine wind" and refers to those who are willing to give their lives to a dangerous cause.) This all-or-nothing attitude is linked to his vow of perfection, and he came to see that he must keep it with utter diligence to be a fit instrument of the Lord. "He, the Lord, is the one who directs; I have nothing else to do but to listen . . . He corrects: I should amend both myself and others."[74]

He expressed his conviction that, if a Jesuit is not prepared to accept the high enterprise of the Society, he should leave. "We should make evident the practical image of the Society today and insist on it, even at the price of losing members who will not adapt themselves to this." He sees as a great danger both naturalism and secularism, ways of thinking that ignore the spiritual or supernatural and which fixate solely on one's own development. He wants to see complete freedom of spirit by which one is fully open "to the action of the Holy Spirit, which is the greatest of all dynamic forces." He is impatient with well-intentioned but narrow interests across the provinces of the Society and wants to see the Society thinking and operating as a global body.[75]

## Yesterday's Answers

In regard to the mission of the Society, Arrupe articulated his fears about the value of the order to a needy world:

> It is not this new world that I am afraid of. What worries me rather is that we Jesuits will have little or nothing to offer it, little or nothing to say to it or do for it that would justify our existence as Jesuits. I am afraid that we may repeat yesterday's answers to deal with tomorrow's problems; that we will speak in such a way that people don't understand us; that we will use a language that does not reach directly to people's hearts. If we do that, then perhaps we will speak more and more, but only to ourselves; nobody else will listen to us, because nobody will understand what we are trying to say.[76]

Many Jesuits, he felt, were afraid of the world: they had been distanced from it as a result of their training, specialization, and emphasis on intellectual rather than practical issues. His challenge to Jesuit alumni to be *for others*, which we will return to later, was relevant also to the Jesuits themselves. The salvation of the whole person, rather than of the soul alone, was his burning concern; he wanted to share with his companions his own passion about contemporary issues: injustice of all sorts, women's rights, the situation of youth, the struggle for faith.

Pedro spoke of a state of desolation among some Jesuits for a variety of factors: hierarchical criticism, the demands of change, a certain loss of common identity, and strong internal divisions. Moreover, the universal call to holiness proclaimed by the Second Vatican Council had undermined the prevailing notion that religious life was in itself a higher state of perfection than marriage. The liberating insight here was that a person didn't have to be a religious to be pleasing to God: the married can be holy too! With this, many who were unhappy in the vowed life left the order and married, leading to a significant drop in vocations in the Society and in other congregations.

Pedro, who had a highly cultivated imagination himself, had the task of liberating the Jesuit imagination, which had atrophied over time in a cramped intellectual environment. He used the image of men stuck in concrete who must be set free to become pliable instruments in divine hands. Ignatius himself had a rich imagination: he used it in praying the Gospel scenes—what we now call imaginative contemplation—and also in the realm of discernment where one has to imagine possible scenarios to which God may be calling. Jesuits were to ask themselves the explosive and imaginative question, What ought I do for Christ? Pedro himself asked this whenever a big issue came up, or, as he put it in his less-than-perfect English, "How to do?" This became an endearing catchphrase echoed by those around him.

Pedro encouraged a more personal style of authority that supported and fostered personal freedom and responsibility, but he would also demand inner growth and openness, as Jesuits grappled with the contemporary world and with the challenge to remain intimately united to Christ. He saw that the less sheltered a Jesuit was, the more he needed to be attached to the Lord. He wanted his companions to experience God, to live with a taste for God; they were to be placed with the Son, as was promised to Ignatius at the Church of La Storta, near Rome, in November 1537.

The importance Arrupe attached to the papacy and to the fulfilling of papal injunctions—for example, combatting atheism—shows, as the editor of his *Retreat Notes* remarks, that if ever the pope had a devoted servant, it was Arrupe—this makes the later failure of trust between the papacy and himself all the more tragic. As an aside, he refused to be called the "black pope," a term used to suggest some hidden power wielded by the Jesuit general over the pope.

Instead Pedro saw himself simply in the role of the pope's servant.

## Jesuit *Aggiornamento*

Pedro did not hesitate to face the challenges emerging in the Church. His primary task as superior general was to preside over the General Congregation that had elected him. The first session of the 31st General Congregation, at which he was elected, had ended before the Second Vatican Council concluded, so Arrupe organized a second session for September–November 1966. This would give delegates a short breathing space to prepare an adequate response to the calls of the Council. It also made for a huge agenda: the revision of the multiple missions of the Jesuits and the updating of the spirit and structures of their religious life. One of the questions debated before his election was whether the person chosen as general "will take to himself what has been begun and proposed by Vatican II, and will encourage this with all his energy."[77] Pedro fulfilled this criterion to the highest degree.

The ecclesiastical scene created by Vatican II was extraordinarily complex: Arrupe had to cope with it at every turn, and there can be no understanding of his work without noting the variety of reactions to the agenda set by the Council. What had happened? The winds of change, resisted for more than a half century, had begun to blow in the Vatican, and across the world there was an emerging sense that the Church must be open to the world, not aloof from it. However, the 2,400 bishops who gathered in Rome in 1962 were, like their flocks, quite unprepared for their task. They thought they would be asked to rubber-stamp the drafts prepared by the Vatican curia, as they had always done before. Instead, they found themselves tasked with leading the Church—belatedly—into the twentieth century. Over three years the bishops hammered out sixteen documents. They then returned home with the daunting challenge of implementing them.

These documents became the immediate agenda for the Society of Jesus, and the second session of the 31st General Congregation was held in the optimistic and hopeful atmosphere generated by the Council. A whole world of freedom and creativity had opened up. A number of the Jesuits present had been expert advisers at the Council and were aware that they were opening a new epoch in the history of their order. The goal was to make operative the Ignatian charism across the world, in fidelity to the Gospels and the Second Vatican Council's work. The sensitive work of *aggiornamento*, or updating, of the Society, focused on internal structures, on spiritual and cultural formation, on ministries, and on the spiritual life of all members. No Congregation achieved more: every aspect of Jesuit life was scrutinized to bring it into line with the original Ignatian charism and to embrace the horizons opened by the Council.

*Structures and Grades:* To update the structures of the Society it was deemed necessary to secure adequate representation of the energy and vision of the younger men at provincial and general congregations: no longer would seniority be the default rule. Also discussed was the leveling of grades within the order, such that all members—and not only the theologically gifted—would be eligible for profession: the complexity of this matter required the establishment of a commission that would report to the next Congregation.

*Formation and Mission:* Formation was to be adapted to prepare young men for a changing world. A personal and deep spirituality would be required, as well as new academic specializations. The emphasis had been on preparing teachers for Jesuit colleges, but with the reevaluation of ministries, new choices had to be made, among them the positive sciences, the world of work, the professions, international organizations, the developing world, the social apostolate, the media. Everything needed to be adapted for service. To all of these and more the pope added the responsibility of combating atheism, in theory and practice.

*Collaboration and Poverty:* Collaboration with the laity began to come to the fore, while apostolic poverty was reaffirmed such that profits from apostolic works such as universities and colleges would no longer go to communities: Jesuits would have to earn what they needed for modest living.

## Ignatian Spirituality

In his search for a common identity for the Society amid its vast diversity and its confusion of vision, Arrupe focused first on the development of Jesuit spirituality. This required much reflection and study, but by carrying it through he recovered for the Society the *Spiritual Exercises of St. Ignatius* in their original one-to-one form. He also commissioned work on the Jesuit *Constitutions* and the *Formula* or "plan of life" of the Institute, both written by Ignatius more than four hundred years earlier but available until then only in Latin and abridged. These three documents were to become the touchstones of the authenticity of a spirituality that had developed accretions over the centuries and lost much of its dynamism.

Each of the three documents would, however, be a dead letter if it did not rely on Divine Providence, on the example of Jesus as given in the Gospels, and on the inspiration of the Holy Spirit. Ignatius had stated clearly: "The Society was not instituted by human means; and it is not through them that it can be preserved and increased, but through the grace of the omnipotent hand of Christ our God and Lord."[78] Pedro restored the Jesuit *Constitutions* by making them accessible in translation, but especially by living them in all his encounters. He was not interested in pushing his own ideas but saw himself as the servant of the Ignatian charism, and he was open to correction on his interpretation of it.

Further, not content with rekindling the heritage of Jesuit spirituality within the order, he opened it to the whole world: it became a rich gift to the universal Church. Prior to Arrupe, Ignatian spirituality had been identified with Jesuit spirituality: if this were so, only Jesuits could live it! Now Jesuit spirituality was recognized as a *particular* and communal mode of living out the broader sweep of Ignatian spirituality. The fact that it had emerged from Ignatius's personal experiences as a layperson trying to find God might explain why Ignatian spirituality finds such enthusiastic reception among laypersons, both Christian and other. In this way, while spearheading the renewal of the Jesuits, Arrupe radically influenced and inspired with Ignatian spirituality many other congregations.

## Corporate Discernment

Corporate discernment came to prominence as Jesuits and their associates engaged in prayerful evaluation of the new needs God may have been asking them to serve. For the Jesuits, choice of residence was to be decided by choice of ministry. They reminded themselves of the statement of Jerónimo Nadal, an early Jesuit: "We are not monks: the world is our house."[79] Jesuit mobility began to reassert itself: remote houses of formation were abandoned in favor of urban locations, guided by the awareness that, whereas St. Benedict loved the heights and St. Bernard the valleys, Ignatius loved the great cities.

Predictability and order within Jesuit houses began to yield to what some called "organized chaos." But this did not disturb Pedro: he was a free spirit who gently but firmly resisted any structure that seemed too confining. One example is well known: during the 1970s a system called "management by objectives" enjoyed considerable popularity. Arrupe was persuaded by his advisers to invite to Rome its designer, an Englishman named John Humble. Humble and his team spent a day skillfully presenting charts showing how the new system could improve the efficiency not only of the Jesuit curia but of the whole Society. In response, Pedro began to explain—at length!—the Jesuit way of proceeding according to the *Spiritual Exercises*, the *Constitutions* and the *Letters of Ignatius*. As he continued, the eyes of the visitors began to roll back further and further into their heads. At the conclusion, John Humble magnanimously said that Ignatius's system of management was marvelous and left nothing to be desired, and really there was nothing in it that should be changed. The curial staff who had hoped that their jobs might have become more streamlined quietly retired to their offices and got on with their work as before.

# 6

# THE CHALLENGE OF RENEWAL

So much for the vision of the 31st General Congregation, but what about its reception on the ground? Pedro could have limited the Society to a notional rather than actual assent to the Second Vatican Council: many bishops were doing just that, and some Jesuits, too. But instead of cautious concessions he embraced the council's full agenda. Here was a major example of the *magis,* understood as the more generous—and more demanding—response. Pedro's criterion was not what the Society could accommodate without significant upheaval, but it was what God wanted done, even if such upheaval followed. Vatican II had ended without timelines or implementation strategies; the ground had not been prepared in advance for its reception across the world. Hence the widespread confusion that ensued over the following half century, of which Cardinal Newman had warned in the wake of Vatican I that we must recollect that there has seldom been a Council not followed by great confusion.

## Second Founder?

More than four hundred years of lived Jesuit history had to be focused on the new world that was emerging. This was how Pedro saw his task. But did this mean that he should be called the re-founder of the order established in 1540? We need to step back to gain perspective on this. Two centuries from its foundation, in 1773, the Jesuit order had been suppressed by Pope Clement XIV. It was restored only forty-one years later, in 1814. The structure of the restored Society was the same as before, but its cultural, political, and even religious mindset reflected the culture of restoration of that period. And unsurprisingly, fear of another suppression led to a conservative approach to the issues of the nineteenth century. So things remained until the twentieth century, when an intensive study of Scripture and ecclesiastical sources began. Within the Society research began to bring to light a deeper understanding of the early Society and its way of proceeding, which was revealed to have been more flexible, more open to fresh challenges, and less moralistic than had been presumed.

Thus, the seeds of *aggiornamento* and of the return by religious congregations to their original inspiration did not come out of the blue but had been gestating for the half century preceding Vatican II. The task for the whole Society was to appropriate the order's original rich identity and focus it on new modes of evangelizing a fast-changing world. Herein lay the continuity with the past, which was a treasure to be mined. This did not mean that Arrupe was refounding the order. His insight was that, as general, Ignatius had exercised his role in a specific period of history and as such must not be followed slavishly. But the founding charism itself is not time bound; it can and must be presented anew in successive periods to remain true to itself. He judged that his task was to focus on Ignatius as founder and to present the charism afresh for a new world. He used to say that he did not want the Society to be led by the general—himself—but by the founder, Ignatius.

> I must first of all follow Ignatius the Founder, and only afterwards Ignatius the General. For there are dimensions of the Ignatian charism which we understand better now [than in Ignatius's day], given the global development of societies.[80]

In his *Retreat Notes* Pedro says, "If St. Ignatius had lived today, he would have founded something different."[81]

# Inertia or Change?

Paul VI was pope from 1963 to 1978: he and the Jesuit general faced the enormous challenge of overcoming ecclesiastical inertia in implementing the agenda of the Second Vatican Council. Passivity had long been imposed on the laity and caution was the password to the hierarchy. The cryptic slogan "Rome has spoken: the case is ended" had silenced opposition and dampened imagination. Those who had enjoyed the status quo continued to justify it by appealing to tradition, and the impatient appealed to Newman's dictum that "to live is to change, and to be perfect is to have changed often." Opposing images of God were at play: is God the unmoved mover of Aristotle or the interventionist God of the Hebrews who likes to surprise humankind by doing new things? In Ireland, the bishops, invoking the plea that "the people are not ready," delayed the introduction of the sign of peace until 1976, and permanent deacons were introduced a full forty years after the Council's decree. More than fifty years later, the implementation of the Second Vatican Council's ideas across the universal Church is still incomplete. Hence the remark of Bernard Lonergan, Jesuit philosopher and theologian, on the Church's "unenviable position of always arriving on the scene a little breathlessly and a little late."[82]

## "God Is Leading Us"

Arrupe's leadership was clear, encouraging, and honest as he faced the mountainous task of renewing and rejuvenating an order with a long and checkered history. He believed in trust and genuine dialogue rather than centralized government. Most deeply he wanted the Society to be led by God. One of his remarks was, "Even if the pilot can't see the port, that's OK!" Often asked, "Where is the Society heading?" he would reply with a twinkle in his eyes:

> Where God is leading it. In other words: I don't know; but there is one thing I do know, and it is that God is carrying us along somewhere. I know that God is leading us towards a new land, the promised land, his land. He knows where it is: our task is only to follow him.[83]

On his great respect for the person, he commented when infirm: "I always wanted to get along with everyone. I can command in only one way. I am not authoritarian. I would explain things to people, and they would have to decide . . . I speak [to the theologians] with simplicity, expressing the way I feel, but I never try to convince them or to force them."[84] This was in line with Ignatius's guidelines. While he sent men on missions across the world with detailed instructions on how to proceed, he would add that they should adjust these in line with local circumstances: imagination, creativity, and discernment were presupposed. Pedro knew that in sending men to the peripheries they would have to experiment and they would make mistakes; the important thing was that spiritual discernment guide their efforts to make the best choices in the given situation.

Pedro became, as we have said, a friend to all Jesuits, and while his great trust in people was doubtless sometimes misplaced, his adult-to-adult dialogical approach was appreciated. Recently I met a Jesuit who when appointed superior asked Arrupe how best to relate to his brethren. Pedro, he said, immediately replied: "Trust your men. Even if you know they will make mistakes, trust them!" Implicit was his awareness that this is how God deals with us fallible human beings, and that we all should do likewise.

The early years of Pedro's leadership flew by, with careful preparation of talks, letters, and interviews, followed by large meetings, press conferences, and intense debate everywhere he went. He had to hold the Society together while it was wracked with growing pains. His incisive comments, his remarkable capacity to read the signs of the times, his sincerity and enthusiasm, were infectious and encouraging, especially to those laboring on the frontiers. It was, however, not surprising that strong divergences of view emerged on the quality of his leadership.

# Institution and Charism

Underlying the widespread friction of the post-Vatican II years was the challenge to combine fidelity to the deposit of revelation with respect for change and development. Herein lies the tension between institution and charism. If that tension is to be life giving, then respect for tradition must be combined with openness to new experiences. Leadership must interpret well the calls of God as proposed by prophetic voices. The impetus to change comes from the Holy Spirit, who is working constantly to renew the face of the earth and gives to particular persons gifts or charisms, which are to be integrated into the life of the Church for its continued growth. Diversity must not bring division, and uniformity must not quench the Spirit.

From Vatican I, in 1870, until Vatican II, however, doctrinal change and development were seen as a threat to an institution that had been shorn of temporal power. In response, papal infallibility was emphasized, and in 1907 came Pius X's condemnation of modernism, understood as the false accommodation of Catholic truth to the subjective spirit of the age. But because change is a constant in human develop ment, prophetic voices asked if the Church should let the world—which is, after all, God's world in process—move ahead without it. With Vatican II emerged the humble image of the pilgrim people of God. Pilgrims are essentially on the move; they have not yet arrived but see themselves as being led into the fullness of truth that Jesus promised.

Many people in the Christian community clung to "the good old days" that seemed to have served them so well. In Ireland, John Charles McQuaid, archbishop of Dublin, fresh from three years at Vatican II, comforted his flock with the following statement: "You may have been worried about much talk of changes to come. Allow me to reassure you. No change will worry the tranquility of your Christian lives."[85] The good archbishop, a highly intelligent man, offered this view while Arrupe was working toward root-and-branch renewal of the Jesuits, which would help the implementation of the vast changes that attended the Church's new growth in self-understanding.

# Pedro and Pope Paul VI

## Atheism

Arrupe's radical obedience to the pope had already been revealed in his response to Pope Paul VI's mandate to the delegates of the 31st General Congregation that they work hard to combat atheism. Called to meet the pope in his early days as general, he began: "The Society is completely at your command. Just give the order, Your Holiness, because obedience is the essence of the Society."

Pedro asked: "With respect to the struggle against atheism, does your Holiness have any concrete suggestion to make to us?" The pope responded: "Yes, but I will say more after the Council."

In his *Retreat Notes* Pedro speaks of secularism and atheism as "the terrible enemies," so it was surprising that in his first press conference after meeting the pope, Pedro stated: "Atheists need to be treated gently, as the Japanese treat the cherry blossom. We must discern in each the reasons that have led them to adopt their position."[86] In the Vatican Council a few days later, to the dismay of many, Arrupe preached a great mobilization against atheism, as an army under the orders of the pope.[87] Pedro showed later a highly nuanced view of atheism, but perhaps he felt obliged by the papal mandate to be less than true to his own convictions.[88] No crusade in fact materialized, but the Society tried to respond sensitively to the issue of contemporary atheism, leading, for example, in Cuba to the accusation that the Jesuits capitulated by opting not for combat but for dialogue with atheists.

## Humanae Vitae

Pope Paul VI's 1968 encyclical on birth control, *Humanae vitae,* caused many good people to abandon the Church, if not the practice of their Catholic faith, and a number of Jesuits queried its reasoning and its authority. Arrupe's letter, written shortly after the encyclical appeared, strongly urges:

"With regard to the successor of Peter, the only response for us is an attitude of obedience which is at once loving, firm, open and truly creative." But he adds:

> To obey is not to stop thinking, nor to parrot the encyclical word for word in a servile manner. On the contrary, it is to commit oneself to study it as profoundly as possible and to rectify our teaching, if need be. The service we as Jesuits owe to the Holy Father and to the Church is at the same time a service we owe to humanity itself.[89]

This letter gave his Jesuit companions plenty for reflection and may have raised questions in the Vatican as to what Pedro meant by being "truly creative." Pedro shared with Ignatius a quasi-mystical view of the popes, and this partly explains why even a passing communication from the pope was so important to him.[90] Arrupe had the theological tendency to blur the distinctions between pope, Rome, Church, and the people of God. Ignatius's own emphasis on the immediate availability of the professed members of the order for the service of the pope, and his *Rules for Thinking with the Church*, also come into play here. Yet Pedro tried to be true to his own convictions.

## Papal Concerns

For the first five years as superior general, Pedro had a trusting and open relationship with Pope Paul VI, who praised his efforts at Jesuit renewal and supported him against his critics. From 1970 onward, however, the pope began to have serious reservations about Arrupe's capacity to curb deviations in writings and teachings that conflicted with the magisterium of the Church. Through Cardinal Villot, his secretary of state, he urged Pedro to make those unpalatable decisions that are inevitably required by good government.

Reports from bishops caused the pope concern: it was alleged that some Jesuits seemed to be abandoning essential elements of the order in favor of a secular mentality. Not all criticisms were wide of the mark. The pope, however, maintained a paternal oversight of the efforts of the Jesuits, not hesitating to criticize those who were neglecting their interior lives or were difficult to govern. In July 1973 Pedro met with Cardinal Villot, as well as Monsignors Benelli and Casaroli. It was a tough meeting, at the end of which Pedro asked for a written summary of the criticisms made so that he could adequately respond to them.

Villot later summarized in a letter the mind of the pope regarding the Jesuits. It began with gratitude for all the good that the Society was doing in the service of the Church but warned of numerous signs of a crisis within the order that would damage the order itself and also other religious institutes. It expressed confidence in the Jesuits' capacity to work through these difficulties and offered the support of the Holy See. Rather than intervening in a drastic way, as he was being urged to do, the pope, according to Villot, much preferred to talk things out with Arrupe. This letter, he said, was to be seen as a new call to action, which year on year was becoming more urgent, since the crisis within the order was being blamed by many as due to a lack of responsible leadership.[91] As we shall see, Pedro tried to win over those in disagreement with the Church's teachings.

# 7

## VISIONARY LEADER

We have been sketching out Arrupe's struggles in ecclesial circles to implement the objectives of the Second Vatican Council. But at the same time, he was busy on many apostolic fronts, offering leadership to those who looked to the Society for help. Keeping in mind that the Jesuit mission is "to help others" and is thus unlimited in its possibilities, we can note some of his initiatives and their challenging vision.

## Men and Women for and with Others

In response to the charge that he was downgrading education in favor of direct work with the poor, Pedro in 1970 proposed education as one of the top four priorities for the Society.

In Mexico, at the 1971 Congress of Jesuit Alumni on education and poverty, he presented "The Schools of the Society, Open to All." The sting was in the final three words. He stated forcefully that the education of the destitute and the marginalized was the responsibility of the whole of society, and he encouraged the alumni to be "the voice of those who have no voice." Then came his famous challenge to Jesuit alumni in Valencia, Spain, in 1973 to share the gift of their education with those at the bottom of the social pyramid.

The occasion was the Tenth International Congress of Jesuit Alumni in Europe. The alumni at that time numbered some two million. Arrupe remarked that probably no address he ever made was so widely circulated or had greater influence in the Society and outside it. True, he said, there were those who hated it and those who loved it: the president of the Spanish alumni resigned in protest, and in many places it was said that the Jesuits had gone communist! Pedro added that he knew his message would offend some in high places, but he felt he had to speak as bluntly as he did.

The original title of the talk was "Men for Others"; this was later amended to "Men and Women for Others." A further amendment followed: "Men and Women for and with Others."[92] What in this address caused such a stir? It was this unequivocal statement:

> Our prime educational objective must be to form men-and-women-for-others; . . . men and women who cannot

even conceive of love of God which does not include love
for the least of their neighbours; men and women completely convinced that love of God which does not issue
in justice for others is a farce.[93]

Arrupe acknowledged that in this area the Jesuits had failed;
conversion of heart was needed if they were to come to the
aid of humankind in its distress and agony. A basic attitude
of respect for everyone was needed, a resolve never to domi-
nate the weak and a willingness to resist all forms of injustice.
He added that Christian education is a call to conversion, to
become fully human by growing in love for all our disadvantaged sisters and brothers. The backdrop to his challenge was
the document of the Synod of Bishops in 1971, which states
that the furthering of justice is a constitutive dimension of
the Lord's mission.

The Jesuits already had educational initiatives specifically
for the poor: in 1955 the Jesuit José Vélaz had established a
new program, Fe y Alegría (Faith and Joy), for Venezuela's
most deprived children. Today, across Latin America, this
program has more than a million children enrolled and uses
sixty-seven radio stations to reach more than two thousand
program centers. Forty years on, in 1995, Jesuit John P. Foley
founded in Chicago the first Cristo Rey (Christ the King)
school for disadvantaged girls and boys, to enable them to
enter university. By working while they study, the students
generate enough funds to keep the school going. Most make

it into higher education and become, in their turn, supporters of the project.

Such initiatives were heartwarming, but Pedro in this address was thinking outside the box and engaging in that seeking of the wider will of God as it emerges in concrete situations. Instead of a Jesuit education that was exclusive and socially advantageous, he was proposing one that was radically inclusive of the disadvantaged, not simply by enabling them to participate thanks to scholarships but by focusing the fruits of that education itself on the service of those in need. Some Jesuit schools would indeed continue to cater to the poor, but all Jesuit schools and higher-level institutions would focus the ambition of their alumni on transforming the lives of the poor.

The Jesuit commitment to education would indeed continue, but the criterion of its excellence would be not academic success alone but the help its alumni would give to the needy of the world. Jesus is the paradigm of the person for others: only by following him do we become fully human.

God's grace calls us to win back not only our whole selves for God but our whole world for God. All of us would like to be good to others, and most of us would be relatively good in a good world. What is difficult is to be good in an evil world.[94]

Half a century on, this challenge remains the underlying agenda for Jesuit educators.

## "All Created Equal"

A letter in 1967 to American Jesuits on the United States' racial issues has become something of a Magna Carta for the worldwide Society in its interracial apostolates. Written in English, with the help of the American provincials, it opens with the challenge posed to the Christian conscience by social discrimination. It links race relations with poverty, quoting from a letter on the Social Apostolate in 1949 by general John Baptist Janssens:

> [Jesuits must understand] what it means to be a member of the lowest class of humankind, to be ignored and looked down on by others; to be unable to appear in public because one does not have decent clothes or the proper social training; to be the means by which others grow rich; to live from day to day on nothing but the most frugal food, and never to be certain about the morrow; to be unable to bring up their children in a decent manner; never to enjoy any decent recreation of soul or body, and at the same time to behold the very people for whom one works abounding in riches, enjoying superfluous comforts, devoting themselves to liberal studies and the fine arts, loaded with honours, authority and praise.[95]

Pedro was challenging, direct, and practical. He appealed to the Declaration of Independence of 1776: "We hold these truths to be self-evident, that all men are created equal, that they are endowed by their Creator with certain inalienable rights, that among these are life, liberty and the pursuit of happiness." He then appealed to Vatican II's repeated condemnation of racism and asked whether the reluctance of American citizens to implement the values of the Declaration of Independence was sadly paralleled by Jesuit hesitation in implementing Christian teaching.

While praising the work of individual Jesuits in the field, the letter required that as a corporate body the Jesuits ask why so little of their effort so far had been expended in work for and with Black people. He suggested the following areas for an examination of conscience:

> An uncritical acceptance of certain stereotypes and prejudices . . . the insulation of far too many Jesuits from the actual living conditions of the poor, and hence of most Negroes; an unconscious conformity to the discriminatory thought and action patterns of the surrounding white community; an unarticulated fear of the reprisals sometimes visited on those who participate in the active Negro apostolate; the mistaken notion that since other priests and religious are serving the Negro, we may exempt ourselves from the obligation of contributing a major effort to the struggle for interracial justice and charity; a lack of sufficient comprehension that the Society . . . is especially committed to the service of Christ's poor.[96]

He asked that his readers reassess their commitments to liberate resources for this work; that Jesuit houses be opened in poor areas to enable young Jesuits to experience the practical problems of the inner city and racial discrimination; that schools adjust intakes accordingly; that vocations be actively fostered among African Americans; and that any discrimination in ministries be totally eliminated.

## The Integrated Life

In late 1976, less than two years after the 32nd General Congregation and its commitment to the integration of faith and justice, Pedro wrote *The Genuine Integration of the Spiritual Life and the Apostolate.* This letter to the whole society addressed a fundamental and perennial challenge to Jesuits: How to integrate work and prayer, so that the service of God and of the neighbor are mutually enriching? How to be contemplative in action? This letter, as is the case with all his addresses, provides insights into Pedro's own life and his relationship with God.[97] This letter was a long time in the making, and its author considered it of special importance to the Society at the time. It is incisive and honest:

> Does our lived spirituality . . . give our apostolic work the creative openness and the daring commitment called for by the 32nd General Congregation, and does our activity reflect a deep spirituality? . . . I am led to pose [these

questions] by this fact: while there is evidence of a spiritual renewal and a new apostolic thrust in the Society, there are nevertheless signs of real deterioration in both areas . . . As a result . . . there is dissatisfaction, personal distaste and disillusion . . . and tensions among individuals and communities . . . One sees apparent fidelity to the practice of traditional manifestations of our spiritual life, but a lack of that apostolic creativity that is needed for the evangelization of the new society in which we live today.[98]

Pedro argues that since our faith and hope live, as it were, outdoors, exposed to the challenges of unbelief and injustice, we need to read all reality from the point of view of the gospel: only in that way can we counteract the secularism, relativism, and denial of the transcendent that are found everywhere. We need abundant contact with God, which we then share generously; our individual and community experiences of prayer should lead us to become captured anew by the call of Jesus Christ.

Communal discernment, revision of life, and theological reflection are helpful, he says, and if at the end of a day or a working session we ask what the Spirit has accomplished in us, what the Lord has wanted to teach us, what we have not done according to the Spirit, then little by little we will learn to look beyond the secular aspects of our work to our specific characteristic as companions of Jesus.

This document made a great impact across the Society, which had already been grappling for the previous ten years with the challenges of renewal. Pedro concludes:

> May the Lord help us to discover in ever-greater depth . . . that spirituality strongly traced out, that robust spirit of St. Ignatius that the pope referred to in his Allocution to the General Congregation . . . There is no other source for our apostolic effectiveness—and that is all that concerns us—than one which is rooted, not in human power, but solely in the strength of God.[99]

## Other Addresses

Pedro wrote a number of other important documents that he hoped might constitute a kind of spiritual legacy. These include "On Apostolic Availability" (1977), "Our Way of Proceeding" (1979), and "Rooted and Grounded in Love" (1981). Taken together, these writings are rich in content, in Scripture citations, and in prayers composed by Arrupe. His contemplative stance emerges: instead of working from principles and coming to logical conclusions, he is inductive, looking realistically at the world around him and at the Society to understand how it might best move forward. For instance, in "Our Way of Proceeding" he describes certain types "who seem less clearly to have the basic elements of the Society's way of proceeding." He calls these types the full-time protestor, the professionalist, the irresponsible, the purely political activist, and the fanatically traditionalist. Obviously, he was speaking from the experience of having to deal with such personalities!

His all-embracing worldview appears again and again. At the Eucharistic Congress in Philadelphia in 1978 he gave the address "Hunger for Bread and the Gospel":

> If, at the end of our discussions . . . as we left the hall, we had to pick our way through a mass of dying bodies, how could we claim that our Eucharist is the Bread of Life? . . . This rediscovery of . . . the social dimension of the Eucharist is of tremendous significance today . . . There was a time when the new land of America was able to say: "Give me your tired, your poor / Your huddled masses yearning to breathe free . . ." Has this great country . . . the courage, the determination, the generosity to give the world the lead it is looking for?
>
> It is only when . . . we give away the little that we have—a few loaves and fishes—that God blesses our poor efforts . . . It was only in sharing their bread with a stranger that the two disciples on the road to Emmaus recognized and found the Lord.[100]

At the 1977 Synod of Bishops, Arrupe pleaded that the Church reach out to people rather than wait for them to come to it; and he insisted once again on enculturation. In the same year, 1977, during the darkest days of conflict in El Salvador, he wrote "Our Recent Five Third World Martyrs":

> Mingled with our deep grief at seeing beloved brothers snatched from our midst is a great happiness . . . [because] through these deaths Jesus Christ has a message for the Society. What is that message? . . . The five were men of average human gifts, leading obscure lives . . . Their style of life was simple, austere, evangelical: it was a life that used them up slowly, day by day, in the service of "the little ones" . . . These are Jesuits of the mold that the world and the Church need today. Men driven by the love of God to serve their brethren without distinction of class or race . . . The thing that counts is that really we resolve to follow Christ even without knowing what sacrifice this following of him will certainly demand of us.[101]

In November 1989, together with their housekeeper and her daughter, six Jesuits were massacred in the garden of the Jesuit residence in San Salvador. They had chosen the preferential option for the poor and paid for it with their lives. Pedro was deeply incapacitated by this time, but he certainly would have offered the same message as he did to the bishops in 1977.

# A Sign of Contradiction

This was Pedro's style: he was never abrasive but was forthright in expressing what should be done. He called things by their names. Inevitably, the local Church frequently opposed such moves and claimed, not entirely unfairly, that some Jesuits, claiming "the spirit of Vatican II," were forging ahead of the Church and becoming a parallel but disobedient Church. This led to frustration among the "movers and shakers" in the Society at not being allowed to meet the real needs of the poor as demanded by Vatican II. At issue was the question of whether Jesuits are to look backward or forward for God's beckoning.

Throughout the 1970s, opposition to Arrupe's vision was relentless: he was charged with encouraging poorly planned experimentation, misinterpreting Vatican II, destroying the Jesuit order, and confusing the faithful. The critics had the ear of the three popes under whom he served: Paul VI, John Paul I, and John Paul II. Pedro endured the soul-testing pain of remaining faithful to Vatican II in a postconciliar Catholic Church that was at best ambiguous about *aggiornamento*.

# 8

# GLOBE-TROTTER

Shortly after taking office, Pedro decided to visit as many of the Jesuit provinces and missions as he could. This arduous mandate was given him by the General Congregation that had elected him, but it was fulfilling for a man who wanted both to learn more about what the Society of Jesus was up to on the ground and to share the challenges of Vatican II and of the recent congregation. He tried to meet all Jesuits and loved to engage in dialogue with them on how best to meet the emerging needs of a new world.

## "If We Are Static, We Die"

In his globe-trotting mission, Pedro visited every continent, and each visit is a study in itself. Everywhere he won the hearts of most of his audience. He began by visiting the Jesuit works around Italy. Next the Near East (Beirut, Baghdad, Damascus); then Africa (Cairo, Addis Ababa, and elsewhere). On his third trip he visited France, where he remarked to the brethren that the Society had no right to be mediocre in the service of God and of people. His fourth voyage, in 1966, was to the United States, including Chicago. It was described as electrifying, as when he said that he feared that Jesuits may be giving yesterday's responses to today's problems. Academic titles, he insisted, are merely helps: if the supernatural does not occupy the primary place, it would be better for us to return to our homes. If the Society remains static, it dies.

In 1967 he visited India, Belgium, Ireland, Alaska, and Canada. In 1968 it was Austria and Yugoslavia, followed by Brazil and Columbia. And so his travels continued: in 1969 he went to Spain and Germany; in 1971 he participated in an ecumenical congress in Dublin; in 1973 he toured Latin America and later participated at the Conference of Latin American Bishops in Puebla in 1979. At the close of the Puebla meeting, a reporter asked him if he had a spare copy of the voluminous text. Arrupe responded: "Yes, I'll gladly let you have mine. But take an aspirin also!"[102] In 1981, after visiting Ireland again, he went to the Philippines and Thailand, then returned to Rome, where his travels came to an abrupt and permanent halt.

# Ireland

Ireland is a microcosm of what Arrupe found in the various Jesuit provinces and how he responded. In June 1967 he first visited an Ireland lauded as having "the best Catholics in the world."[103] But the country was dominated by an atmosphere of episcopal caution toward the world and lay initiatives. Instead, blind faith and passivity were commended. "Pay up. Pray up. Shut up!" was the cynical joke of the day.

Although the crowded schedule of receptions, speeches, homilies, and meals was essentially intended for meetings with 450 Irish Jesuits, the country took notice of Pedro's arrival. He met with members of the government and the hierarchy, and with Jesuit associates. President Eamon de Valera declined his invitation only because of illness. An *Irish Independent* editorial, headed "Distinguished Visitors," said that it was surely a sign of the times that the archbishop of Canterbury and the general of the Society of Jesus were visiting Ireland the same weekend, and that Ireland was clearly of interest to the Christian world beyond its shores.

# Change and Confusion

In Ireland Pedro met a confused band of Irish Jesuits. As obedient men, the elders had supported deeply the pre-Vatican II Catholic Church; any criticism of it appeared a disloyalty. Cecil McGarry, who became provincial in 1968, stated that few of his Irish Jesuit brethren of that period felt needed in the Church; rather, they saw themselves as part of a machine. They did what they were told and had little opportunity to express their dreams. He went on:

> My lowest point in these years was the Provincial Congregation of 1970. I went into it with trepidation yet considerable hope. But it turned out to be largely a looking backward rather than forward, a resistance to change, a defence of the status quo, a desire to see the arrival point clearly before taking a first step into the unknown. No movement could be made as long as people were full of fear and unable to express their fears, desires or anger at what was going on.[104]

The younger men yearned for openness and inspiration but could not find it. They queried whether their communities were places of mutual support, understanding, acceptance, and openness. If not, why stay in them? The province that Pedro addressed was thus a divided one, a microcosm of the worldwide Society. What had he to say to such an audience?

## An Eye to Social Justice

He had come, Arrupe said, to meet with Irish Jesuits "so that the Society I serve can serve Ireland better." He noted appreciatively that 20 percent of Irish Jesuits were working overseas and stressed the need for those at home to update all their ministries with an eye to social justice, using the global social survey he had initiated. The Society was by preference to serve the poor, even at the price of abandoning works that were good in themselves but did not help the disadvantaged. Irish Jesuits would, he admitted, need courage to move in this way. Alms were not enough: the Jesuits must enable everyone they served to develop to the fullness of their personality. It must not be said of the Jesuits: "You preach a very fine-sounding doctrine, but only the socialists and the communists have improved our condition." He was both encouraging and challenging: he spoke of the need "to get out of the cement" in order to serve a fast-changing world:

> Our Society has a great future, but we must become elastic. You have chosen in Christ to serve a world in movement that needs to be put in contact with his personality. If you stop, you say "no," not only to the world but to Christ who goes onward with the world.[105]

He met with parents of Jesuits and brought tears from the mothers, including my own, when he acknowledged their generosity in giving their sons to the Society; he left the fathers a bit miffed, however, at the fact that *their* sacrifice was not mentioned! That he had a soft spot for mothers was revealed when he brought back to a young Jesuit studying in Rome a message from his Irish mother to write more often!

When told by parents that the Jesuit curia in Rome was forbidding, he quipped: "You're always welcome. We're not cannibals, you know!"

# A Time of Suffering

Pedro made three further trips to Ireland: in 1971, 1978, and 1981. In 1971 he came to Dublin to open the Fourth International Congress of Jesuit Ecumenists and found time to update the province on the current state of the Society. His mood was more somber than before: he spoke of a time at Gethsemane but also of the sure hope of resurrection. Problems were to be seen as challenges; inner freedom was needed to let go the past and embrace the new horizons into which God was beckoning. He expressed gratitude for the honest expression of differences of opinion about the spiritual health of the province. While overall numbers in the order had indeed declined by about four thousand, he said that what was most important was that Pope Paul VI looked to the Society with great hope and affection. He asked those in formation for their commitment to the intellectual apostolate and to familiarity with the history of the Society. He was departing, he said, with a sense of supernatural confidence and optimism: "If God is for us, who can be against us?" He would return to the grounds for his optimism later: "Yes, I am optimistic, and I will tell you why: because God works over the long haul."[106]

He came again in April 1978, was warmly received, and gave addresses on the role of local superiors, on the challenges for our educational apostolate, on formation, and on the internationality of the Society. I was his host in Milltown Park at the time, and in an aside, when I asked him about how things were going with the Holy See, he paused, smiled, and said: "On the one hand things are terrific: . . . on the other hand, things are not so good!" The following year I met him in Rome as a member of a delegation that was proposing to set up the Dublin University School of Theology in partnership with Trinity College. He was enthusiastic about the initiative but reminded us as we were departing that the key factor would be the approval of the Catholic archbishop. The acronym for the project—DUST—turned out to be all too accurate.

## Final Visit

Arrupe's last visit to us was in June 1981, when he met first with those involved in formation, then with two hundred brethren. I recall how he was at his enthusiastic best and that he made no less an impression than he had in 1967. We felt flattered that with his worldwide concerns he could take the time to visit us yet again. He blessed the site of the new nursing unit at Cherryfield Lodge in Dublin, a symbol of the phenomenon of aging that was emerging across the Society. Within two months Pedro himself would be in nursing care in Rome, never to recover. He was genuinely loved and admired and left good memories behind him. Few of those who met him left his presence without feeling more spring in their step. They felt that he was interested in them as persons as well as in their work, their prayer, and their challenges. His authority was natural, not assumed. He had no airs and graces but was direct, sincere, unassuming. In sketching his spirituality earlier, I borrowed the phrase "luminous transcendence," which shone out from him. Just as Jesus came to bring life, so did Pedro.

# 9

# DIARY OF A GENERAL

## Daily Routine

Arrupe attended community meals in the curia—though he ate very frugally—loved company at table and was a lively conversationalist. From his time in Japan he had developed the habit of taking a hot bath in the afternoon. He had no exercise regime and took no holidays. He had the ability to take catnaps: a quarter of an hour in the car while being driven away from a heavy meeting was enough to refresh him for the next one. With the permission of his driver, he practiced "prayer on the go" or "noisy contemplation." As Jesus lived his busy days without losing sight of his Father, so did Pedro: he was neither lost in a disconnected spirituality nor cynical about the state of the world. Instead, he lived out of an unquestioning conviction that God is everywhere at work, orchestrating the chaos of human affairs.

## A Prayer-Filled Life

It has been said that the more you have to do, the more you need to pray! On my wall is my favorite portrait of Pedro: black-gowned, kneeling in a Zen-like posture, absorbed in silent prayer. His sandals are beside him, a symbol of the fact that in this sacred time he is not on the move, physically or mentally. No matter how pressing his affairs, he is giving over that precious period to God alone. He remarked that when feeling stressed, he found Zen helpful, with its emphasis on silent presence.

Those close to him would study his face when he came to table, wondering what might have gone on between God and their general in his "little cathedral" early in the morning—rather like the Israelites who stood at their tents when Moses emerged from encountering God in the tent of meeting (Exodus 33:7–11).

He was one of those people whose life would make no sense if God did not exist. "God is all," he would say. "All my time is at the service of the Society."[107] He rose between 4:00 and 4:30 in the morning and spent three hours in prayer. During that time, he celebrated Mass alone in his small chapel, and he would also join in the afternoon community

Mass. Given the opportunity, which was rare enough, he would spend up to four hours celebrating alone. He also prayed as he journeyed, practiced the reflective pauses or "checking-in periods," which in Ignatian spirituality are known as the Daily Examen, and gave time to quiet prayer before retiring.

There is the story of a novice asking him, "How much time do you give to prayer, Father?" Pedro launched into a homily on the importance of prayer for a Jesuit. But the novice was brave and insisted: "Father, how many hours do *you* pray every day?" Silence. Then: "About four hours." More silence. Then he added, "But in that time I also offer Mass and say part of the Divine Office. And of course, one needs to be talking with God all the time. Isn't that what Ignatius says?"

One of my brethren in Dublin was living next to our visitor's room when Pedro showed up. Knowing the story about the four hours' prayer, he decided not to let the Irish province down, so he set his alarm for 3:55, ran the taps noisily, got back into bed, and woke up in time for breakfast!

## Talking with God

Arrupe's remark about "talking with God all the time" indicates that he had made his own Ignatius's discovery that God is at play in our inner world and can be found in our feelings and moods, our likes and dislikes. By pausing in the day to notice what is going on inside, Pedro was tracking the path of the Spirit and learning where he was being led. Ignatius had developed this spirituality of the heart to the point that, as he admits in his *Reminiscences*, "he was always growing in ease in finding God, and every time and hour he wanted to find God, he found him."[108] Jerónimo Nadal, Ignatius's earliest interpreter, held strongly that the graces given to Ignatius were meant for those who embraced his spirituality. Pedro experienced the truth of this: his waking hours seem to have been immersed in the divine. One of my senior brethren hinted at the same experience, remarking that he found it hard to speak about his prayer as distinct from his ordinary life. He said, "Either I'm praying all the time or I'm not praying at all!"

What else can be said of Pedro's ways of being in touch with the divine? Perhaps he would have echoed Elizabeth of the Trinity's response when asked what she did in prayer. She said that the divine Persons and herself spent their time loving one another! He also brought his problems to his divine confidants. Talking once to writers who were dismayed by ecclesiastical criticism, he said:

> What is to be done then? Well, sit down before Jesus Christ, in your house chapel. Place yourself before Christ abandoned in Gethsemane. Leave everything there—your

person, your things, everything. And then you will feel free, totally free.[109]

He returned to the same point later:

> I speak to [the theologians] with simplicity . . . But I never try to convince them or force them . . . The attitude of silencing or severely censoring is harmful. I have got along very well with the theologians, for example with Karl Rahner . . . They can be requested to . . . change their styles. But in the present situation silence is imposed, as happened with Teilhard and de Lubac. You have to obey and have faith.[110]

Elsewhere he speaks of his own intimate conversations with God, without which he would not be able to continue, much less bear the burden of his responsibilities.[111]

## "Here I Am, Lord!"

As a Jesuit I have made an annual eight-day retreat over some sixty years. Sometimes the retreat "took off," but frequently enough I entered it without any great enthusiasm and exited it without having had a transformative experience. I have long forgotten how I felt in making my retreat in 1965, but from the same year we have the *Retreat Notes* that Arrupe wrote immediately after becoming general. They are titled: *"Aqui me tienes, Señor!"* "Here I am, Lord" (or literally, "Here

you have me, Lord"). Either way, it has strong biblical resonances, hinting at the cry of the young Isaiah who is overwhelmed by divine glory in the temple (Isaiah 6:1–8). It also
echoes Jeremiah's admission: "You have seduced me, Lord,
and I have let myself be seduced" (Jeremiah 20:7).

The phrase "Here I am, Lord" speaks of Pedro's unlimited
openness to and enthusiasm for whatever God wishes. It
expresses his lifelong inner stance before the divine, and it is
repeated in his final testament in 1983: "More than ever I
find myself in the hands of God. This is what I have wanted
all my life from my youth."[112] It makes me blush now when
I contrast Pedro's attitude of heart with my own!

The *Retreat Notes* are intensely personal: they spark reve-
lations about his relationship with God, as sketched at the
beginning of this book. But Pedro's preoccupation is with the
developing of schemes and strategies that he will need in fulfilling his new mandate as general. Here is the mystic with
open eyes, gazing on the world, and planning with God how
he can best serve it. His *Retreat Notes* are a working document, almost a communal discernment with God on a variety of topics. Head and heart interplay as he tries to grasp the
continuous creative action of God.

His deep fidelity to Ignatius is a constant feature:

This creative activity of each moment. Lord, let me feel
this, as you gave St. Ignatius to feel it! . . . If we are to

follow the example of St. Ignatius, we have to see how he fought and proceeded against the evils of his time.[113]

This is the "younger Pedro" at the height of his powers: his remarkable intelligence shines through as does his magnanimity, his greatness of soul, his enthusiasm, his dynamic energy that would inspire all his ventures as general. The years that follow will mellow him further, but already he has a dim sense of his impending passion. He writes:

> The one thing that remains forever and in every place, which has to orientate me and help me always, even in the most difficult circumstances, and in the face of the most painful misunderstandings, is always the love of the sole friend who is Jesus Christ.[114]

## Mystic with Open Eyes

Pedro never referred to himself as a mystic, but as we noted above, he prayed to have a mystic's eyes: "Grant me, O Lord, to see everything now with *new eyes*. Give me the clarity of understanding that you gave St. Ignatius."[115] This grace was richly given him because he viewed the world with eyes focused on the new directions set by the Vatican Council. He saw himself as an utterly poor man who was trying to respond to the daily inspirations of God that he was experiencing. From our opening chapters in this book, it is clear that the main actors in his life were the divine Persons, so that his life was a living experience of God's presence and action. He encountered God both in prayer and in all of life's events. This is enough to affirm that he was a mystic.

In 1971 Karl Rahner helped to ground mysticism in ordinary experience: "The devout Christian of the future will either be a 'mystic,' one who has experienced 'something' or will cease to be anything at all . . . The primary and essential factor, and one which must play a decisive role in the Christian living of the future also, is one's direct personal relationship with God."[116] By "experience" he means that one has moved beyond an intellectual grasp of the faith to a felt awareness of the Mystery that lies within daily existence and points to the beyond. This affirmation struck a chord in the hearts of "ordinary Christians" and gave them the belief that there is, in fact, no glass ceiling between them and those who would find their names in McGinn's seven-volume *History of Western Mysticism*. Further, with Pope Francis's 2015 encyclical *Laudato si*, mystical intimacy with God is shown to be accessible to every human being, through creation, because "everything is, as it were, a caress of God . . . There is a mystical meaning even in a leaf or a poor person's face . . . He [God] comes to us from within, so that we might find him in this world of ours."[117] Thus, while Lamet helpfully lists Pedro's "mystical experiences," these must be seen *within* rather than *beyond* the context of his daily life. Those who labor to find God in all things are in fact meeting God at every hand's turn, whether or not they realize this to be so!

## "How to Do?"

Arrupe's working day when at home was given over to prayer, discernment, planning with his advisers, reading, study and reflection, writing letters, and preparing addresses and interviews. Thus he followed the daily regime proposed for the general by Ignatius in the 1540s: "the general should spend his day partly with God, partly with his staff, and partly with himself in deciding what should be done with God's help."[118] We note how for Ignatius God is the first port of call!

Arrupe traveled the world, as we have seen, to meet his Jesuit brethren and to attend conferences. While he always booked an economy seat, airline staff often moved him to first class, perhaps with prompts from those who looked after him. He traveled with a very small bag but often imaginative gifts for those he was to meet. His outer surroundings seemed to have little impact on him; we rarely hear of the cherry blossoms of Japan, the beauty of the great oceans, or the fine foods sometimes set before him. There is the story of his journeying in the Middle East when the great pyramids suddenly came into view. One of his companions could not repress an exclamation of amazement: Pedro looked, nodded, and then immediately turned back to his conversation about the apostolic challenges that Jesuits faced in Egypt.[119]

But whatever was human found resonance with him. He loved fun and liked to get his brethren laughing. His jokes were always made with good humor, as when he was asked, "How are your relations with Monsignor X?" He responded: "Fine, though he must like me less now, because before he used to give me two kisses, and now he gives me just one!" He was a good imitator and would represent with words and gestures attitudes and postures thought to be typically Jesuit. He was an excellent singer: he would sing Basque and German songs, followed by a duet in Japanese. Then, with one of his aides he would sing the African American spiritual "Nobody Knows the Trouble I've Seen"—which he jokingly referred to as his theme song, because, he claimed, it told his own story.

## Eucharist

In Arrupe's devotion to the Eucharist he again resembled Ignatius, who would often take hours to celebrate. We have noted that when in solitary confinement for thirty-three days in Japan, Arrupe's greatest suffering was to be deprived of the Eucharist, which he said was the center of his life, the most important act of his entire daily routine. I recall how upset he became when some younger Jesuits began to question not only the relevance of devotion to the Sacred Heart but also the value of the daily Eucharist. "Wouldn't weekly Eucharist suffice?" they asked. The issue reveals that he could get seriously upset over things close to his heart. He wove his concern about the Eucharist not into a tirade but into a personal reflection:

> Lord, without the Mass my life would remain empty and my strength would weaken. However, I hear that some of our men are so unconcerned about your presence in the tabernacle that they do not pay even one visit to you during the day . . . They recognize the infinite value of the Mass but they say that it is excessive to celebrate such a tremendous reality every day. And they maintain that they should not celebrate if there is no community present . . . I do not doubt their good will, their subjective truth, but I do not understand it. Lord, enlighten us: Lord, teach me your ways. (Psalm 25:4)[120]

This prayer shows the strength of his own devotion to the Eucharist, as well as his willingness to change his position if shown he should do so. Significantly, he did not publish this reflection for a number of years out of sensitivity to the brethren with whom he was at odds.

One of his Benedictine friends acknowledged that, while Arrupe couldn't be given high grades for liturgical awareness, his sense of the transcendent always shone through. At his Masses one knew that a holy man was presiding.

Not only was the Eucharist so important to him personally, but it had for him a cosmic significance. Shortly after his arrival in Japan in 1938, Pedro and a Jesuit brother climbed Fujiyama, Japan's sacred mountain. A hard climb of eleven thousand feet, it had to be done by four in the morning; by six, the peak would be covered in cloud. He described what happened:

> My mind was bubbling with a great number of projects for the conversion of the whole of Japan . . . The climb had been most tiring, but once we had reached the top the sight of the rising sun was stupendous . . . Above us was the blue sky, below us eighty million people who did not know God. My mind ranged out beyond the lofty vaulting of the sky to the throne of the divine majesty. I seemed to see Jesus and with him St. Francis Xavier, the first apostle of Japan, whose hair had become white within a few months because of the sufferings he had to endure . . . If I had known then how much I would have to suffer, my hands would have trembled as I raised the sacred host. On that summit so near to heaven I understood better the mission with which God had entrusted me . . . I could repeat with more conviction the words of Isaiah: "Here I am, send me!"[121]

There are echoes here of the experience fifteen years earlier of Pierre Teilhard de Chardin, who on Easter Sunday in 1923 sat under a tree in the Ordos Desert of Inner Mongolia. As the sun came up, he wrote the mystical essay "Mass on the World":

> *With neither bread, nor wine, nor altar, I your priest will make the whole earth my altar and on it will offer you all the labours and sufferings of the world. Once again Fire has penetrated the Earth. No visible tremor marks this transformation; and yet, at the touch of your Word the immense host, which is the universe, is made flesh. Through your incarnation, my God, all matter is henceforth incarnate.*[122]

This theme of the universal scope of the Eucharist has penetrated deeply into Catholic thought. Pope Francis says in *Laudato si*:

> The Eucharist is an act of cosmic love: yes, cosmic, because even when it is celebrated on the humble altar of a country Church, the Eucharist is always in some way celebrated on the altar of the world.[123]

# 10

# THE STRUGGLE FOR JUSTICE

Given the extraordinary complexity of the Catholic Church and the world it was being called to serve, modes of corporate governance were proposed at the Second Vatican Council that would work in the spirit of collegiality that grew out of the council. Shortly after, in the teeth of opposition from the Vatican's old guard, Pope Paul VI brought in two related reforms: the creation of the Synod of Bishops, which would meet every two or three years to advise the pope, and the establishment of regional collegial bodies of bishops worldwide. The Synod of Bishops, chosen from the worldwide episcopate on a rotating basis, would meet regularly to advise the pope on how to implement the conciliar decrees. It was widely presumed that this body would take precedence over the various Roman congregations responsible for the affairs of the Church heretofore. The national episcopal councils would foster subsidiarity, help decentralize the Church, and reform the papacy. However, these hopes turned out to be wide of the mark.

## The 1971 Synod

The synods began in 1967 and in 1971 dealt with two topics: ministerial priesthood and justice in the world. The first document praised priests for the dedication to their ministry and noted the challenges they faced. The second document broke new ground:

> Action on behalf of justice, and participation in the transformation of the world, fully appear to us as a constitutive dimension of the preaching of the Gospel; or in other words, of the Church's mission for the redemption of the human race and its liberation from every oppressive situation.[124]

This is breathtaking! For those open to facing the vast injustices in the world it was an awesome and stirring challenge. Holding on to the faith is not enough, and preaching the gospel without engaging with the reality of peoples' lives is not enough: preaching and action must go together, or else the Church's commitment to the modern world is paper thin. The document *Justice in the World* sketched out what the

Second Vatican Council had affirmed six years earlier: the joys and hopes, the grief and anguish, of the people of our time, especially those who are poor or afflicted, are the joys and hopes, the grief and anguish, of the followers of Christ as well.

As a loyal servant of the Church, Arrupe endorsed the vision behind the document and pondered what it should mean for the Society of Jesus. The issue would not go away: the Good News brought by Jesus involves an unwavering commitment to justice for his people. In the history of the Hebrews, God is shown as the liberator of the oppressed, the one who casts the mighty from their thrones and raises the lowly. Jesus himself opposed every form of domination: of children, women, outcasts, lepers, foreigners, sinners, even the possessed and those overcome by the power of death. True love of others implies standing with them in their oppression, as the parable of the good Samaritan illustrates: in its closing line we are told, "Go and do likewise" (Luke 10:37). The Gospel indeed comforts the afflicted but afflicts the comfortable. Preaching on justice and denouncing oppression have their place, but they ring hollow unless matched by engagement in the actual struggle for justice. As one of my professors used to say, "There are no armchairs on Calvary"!

# Justice in the Church

The synod of 1971 went even further: there must, it said, be justice not only in the world but also within the Church. This is spelled out in a searching examination of conscience for the Church itself:

- Those who speak to others about justice must first be seen to be just themselves.

- Within the Church the rights of everyone, male and female, must be defended.

- The Church recognizes everyone's right to suitable freedom of thought and expression and their right to be heard in a spirit of dialogue which preserves a legitimate diversity in the Church.

- The members of the Church should share in the drawing up of decisions.

- Positions of privilege must not obscure evangelical witness; the lifestyle of all members of the Church must be examined; belonging to the Church must not place people on a rich island within an ambience of poverty.

Arrupe had attended the 1971 synod as president of the Union of Superiors General, which included 220 religious congregations with a global membership of more than a million women and some three hundred thousand religious men. He had intervened three times, giving two speeches on priesthood and the third on the Church's contribution to justice in the world. We may believe that his own values shine out through the text. He had pleaded for rapid, effective, courageous, and universal action by the Church; for the formation of men and women who would be authentic agents of social change—people gifted with a sense of the universal who know how to read the signs of the times and are capable of serving humankind well. When queried as to whether the Church should denounce specific injustices, he stated his belief that that is the duty of the local Church, while the universal Church should express solidarity in cases of well-documented injustices. He also defended Pope Paul VI, stating that no one could do, or in fact had done, more for justice than he had.

## Vatican Reaction

Under Arrupe's leadership as general, the popes Paul VI, John Paul I, and John Paul II presided over a variety of responses and reactions to the Second Vatican Council, with each trying to bring about interior conversion to its vision. In contrast to the popes, of course, Arrupe enjoyed the advantage of having only a small and reasonably cohesive group to work with, whereas Catholics worldwide numbered over a billion and covered a vast spectrum. For members of the hierarchy who were already unhappy about the reforms of

Vatican II, *Justice in the World* brought further concern. The proposed linking of justice with the proclamation of the gospel, the self-examination by the Church on its own internal witness to justice, the proposal that women should have appropriate responsibility and participation in the life of the Church—these and many more proposals were perceived as threatening to men who yearned for a return to a pre-Vatican II Catholic Church.

The 1971 document was largely greeted by silence in Vatican circles. For many, it was a bridge too far and would have required a deep level of conversion and power sharing within the Church, so it was quietly shelved and allowed to fade away from ecclesial consciousness into the limbo of unwanted reports. Fifty years on, it is absent from the Vatican's monumental *Compendium of the Social Doctrine of the Church*. Of those wedded to power, comfort, safety, social status, and upward mobility, it asked too much. It was subversive, dangerous. Some in the Vatican queried the very existence of a Synod of Bishops drawn from the corners of the earth: surely, for the order of the Church to survive, the emphasis must be on the papacy and the pronouncements of Rome's centralized institutions. The outcome was that synods continued but were forbidden to issue statements of their own; instead, the pope of the day would write a post-synodal exhortation.

Despite the initial reaction, *Justice in the World* is still relevant. In its own way it is a watershed document, and perhaps its time has come with Pope Francis's call for a synodal Church, in which the whole people of God, led by the Spirit, would walk together and converse with the Lord, as the disciples did on the road to Emmaus.

## The Jesuits and Justice

As for Arrupe, he embraced the spirit of the document. Commitment to the poor, the dispossessed, and the marginalized was already an integral part of his personal and Christian development. He had experienced many situations of injustice, such as the slums of Madrid, expulsion from Spain, imprisonment in Japan, and the carnage of Hiroshima; he had contributed to the Council's debate on the role of the Church in world affairs. Thus his dream was to focus all Jesuit resources and works on the promotion of faith and justice, and he worked tirelessly to gain support for his vision. He said that faith is one hand and justice the other, and we do our most constructive work when we use both. But, given that the Church was largely unready for this revolutionary view of evangelization, he acknowledged that the struggle to link faith and justice would be one of the greatest challenges to the Society.

How did the Society move forward? Study of *Justice in the World* led to lively exchanges and contrary views among Jesuits. These ranged from "How can we go about this, given that our focus has been mainly on the service of the faith?" to "What about Ignatius's comment that love is to be found in deeds rather than in words?"

## Leadership

Here again Arrupe's leadership was decisive: given the stark clarity of the synodal document, he held that another Congregation should be convened, both to confirm the decisions made a decade earlier in the 31st General Congregation and to review in the light of experience how best to serve the world and the Church into the future. Criticism of the Jesuits' approach to *aggiornamento* was being supported by members of the Vatican curia and by members of the Society itself, and this negativity from within was not lost on the Society's enemies in Rome. Pedro himself took it to heart and decided that the Jesuits must face it head-on to discern communally how God wanted the order to proceed.

Arrupe was honest and fearless. He knew that this "fundamental option" would demand yet a deeper change and conversion on the part of the Society than ever before. In 1983, during his sickness, he revealed that in the early 1970s he had sensed himself being led to a new depth of discipleship:

In 1973 I saw clearly that something completely new was beginning. I was interiorly certain. I didn't have the least doubt that I had to travel by a new road. What a beautiful experience it was! I told this to the Jesuits gathered in Rome for a meeting, and they agreed to convoke the general congregation. The Jesuits had to come to terms with something new.[125]

Commenting on the outcome of the 32nd General Congregation, he stated:

In the light of this option, the Congregation expects us to re-evaluate our apostolic links and commitments. We have to make an Ignatian discernment, with all that this implies. This is clearly much more demanding and requires deeper changes in the life and activity of the Society. But it is indispensable if we are to remain relevant and retain the role we have always had of being shock troops in the front line of the apostolate.[126]

# 11

# THE 32ND GENERAL CONGREGATION, 1974–1975

## Resignation?

Before the 32nd General Congregation began in December 1974, it was clear that the approval or rejection of Pedro's leadership style would be an important issue. Rumor had it that he would resign because of opposition from within, or that the pope might move to suppress the Society. But from the beginning the more than two hundred delegates gave overwhelming approval to the direction in which Pedro was leading the Society. He, the ever-imaginative optimist, was willing to risk anything good for the sake of God's Kingdom and was still the darling of the media: he made the front cover of *Time* in April 1973.

## Faith and Justice

The congregation itself is centrally remembered for its statement "Our Mission Today: The Service of Faith and the Promotion of Justice." This decree, addressing the whole Society, took as its foundation the key statement of the 1971 Synod of Bishops: "Action on behalf of justice, and participation in the transformation of the world, fully appear to us as a constitutive dimension of the preaching of the Gospel." Thus the Jesuit document, known as Decree 4, states: "The mission of the Society of Jesus today is the service of faith, of which the promotion of justice is an absolute requirement."

The decree was passed only on the last day, but with overwhelming support. Justice was seen to embody God's love for the world. But the costs were foreseen: the loss of friends and support, opposition, and death. This last has been amply verified: between 1973 and 2014 some 53 Jesuits died violently because of their dedication to justice. Opting for the least and the last meant sharing their fate. One Jesuit commented after the murder of a fellow Jesuit: "Freedom is not free: it has to be paid for with one's life," and this prophetic remark found its way into the final text, which included the statement that "any effort to promote justice will cost us something: our cheerful readiness to pay the price will make the preaching of the Gospel more meaningful."

## Solidarity with the Poor

Making the promotion of justice an absolute requirement in the service of the gospel was new and disruptive. Within the Society, we "at the peripheries" struggled to grasp and implement its implications. Some men chose to live in poorer areas to share to some degree the poverty of those around them. Others had to think outside the box to see how to bring their middle-class structures in line with the decree. This involved discussion, prayer, disagreement, and compromise. I was superior of a large house of studies during the 1970s: numbers dropped from eighty-five to fifty-six in the community as deinstitutionalization took hold. With more or less discernment, the younger men—and some older men—went to live in small communities. Our Institute of Theology and Philosophy opened its doors to the laity, offered bursaries to the needy, and reconfigured courses to raise staff and student consciousness of the reality of injustice in God's world.

The whole range of our apostolic works was reevaluated in the light of the decree. The Centre of Jesuit Spirituality in Dublin was critiqued as strong on faith but silent on justice. To remedy this, experiences among the poor were proposed to intending retreatants to help them convert to the radicality of Jesus' message. The novitiate was relocated from its isolated rural setting to a parish serving a disadvantaged population, and novices were tested on their ability to engage in the struggle for justice and warned that such work was not for the fainthearted. As Arrupe's successor, Peter-Hans Kolvenbach, emphasized:

> This very mission has produced martyrs [as in El Salvador] who prove that "an institution of higher learning and research can become an instrument of justice in the name of the Gospel. But implementing Decree 4 is not something a Jesuit university accomplished once and for all. It is rather an ideal to keep taking up and working at . . . A conversion to keep praying for . . ." The beautiful words of GC 32 show us a long path to follow: "The way to faith and the way to justice are inseparable ways. It is up this undivided road, this steep road, that the pilgrim Church . . . must travel and toil. Faith and justice are undivided in the Gospel which teaches that 'faith makes its power felt through love.' They cannot therefore be divided in our purpose, our action, our life."[127]

In *Ex corde ecclesiae* in 1990, Pope John Paul II defined the characteristics required in third-level institutions that wished to be called Catholic: he charged them with the safeguarding of human dignity and the promotion of justice for all. This agenda is similar to that taken up by Arrupe in 1973, when he defined the ultimate goal of Jesuit education as the preparation of its alumni to serve those in need.

## Profession for All?

The topic of grades within the Society might not seem important today, but because it led to a difficult struggle between the Vatican and the Society, we need to ask what it was all about and how Arrupe misread papal signals, with unfortunate consequences.

The issue of grades began early on. St. Ignatius had structured the Society of Jesus hierarchically, which was not seen as unusual in the 1540s. At the top were those who at their final profession were given four vows: in addition to the common vows of poverty, chastity, and obedience, they took a fourth vow of obedience to the pope in regard to availability for mission anywhere in the world. These were named "the professed" and were the inner core of the Society: posts of greater responsibility were assigned to them. Next came the spiritual coadjutors, priests whose task was to assist the professed: they took the three vows. Last came the temporal coadjutors, who were known as brothers, had three vows, and were not ordained. But four hundred years after Ignatius's time, the world had changed, and many Jesuits wanted an end to the concept of first- and second-class members, because it clashed with the gospel call to equality and justice and ran counter to Vatican II. It was also argued that the criteria for profession were biased toward intellectual ability, as tested by a theology examination, which led to men otherwise eminently suitable for the Society's most important tasks being passed over.

The distinction between grades was in fact falling into disuse in practice, but juridically it remained. The Church had called for the appropriate updating of religious life in all its forms, and in consequence, the 31st General Congregation had mandated a study of the issue of profession, to be presented to the following congregation.

## "Let the Matter Not Be Treated!"

Early on, the Vatican advised Arrupe that any proposal to equalize the grades in the Society presented grave difficulties that would prevent the Holy See from giving the necessary approval. In Vatican terminology, this meant: "Let the matter not be treated." But the delegates voted to discuss the matter, invoking the Jesuit custom of allowing its members to make representation to superiors of their views on important matters before a final decision was taken. The delegates thus believed that it was acceptable for them to represent to the Holy Father their carefully discerned view on equality in the Society, leaving the final decision to him. For his part, Arrupe understood that because a General Congregation is the highest legislative body in the Society, he as general must allow it to decide its own agenda and procedure.

So a protracted debate ensued, with Cardinal Villot frequently warning Arrupe that the Society was moving in the wrong direction. Finally on February 20, 1975, Arrupe went to the papal apartments to clarify what the pope expected of the delegates, and at the same time to assure the pope of the Jesuits' goodwill. The pope was surprised that his desire to exclude all debate on grades had not been understood from the start. A key factor for his stance was that the Jesuit vow of obedience for papal missions seemed to him to be in jeopardy. Such availability obviously was highly valued by the popes, and because Pope Paul considered it an essential point of the Formula of the Jesuit Institute, he said that the Society must remain faithful to its founding vision and make no change. In the Jesuit view, however, the abolition of grades would not have diminished but extended the number of Jesuits available to the pope for whatever missions he wished to assign them.

## Pedro's Apology

As noted earlier, Pedro was deeply distressed by the tone of the meeting but immediately communicated its outcome to the waiting delegates. A later papal letter confirmed that no innovation could be introduced with regard to the fourth

vow. Drawing on his reserves of self-control and inner freedom, Pedro invited the delegates to celebrate the Eucharist,
during which he gave a homily on "obeying with joy." He
took responsibility for the misunderstanding with the pope,
saying that it was due not to lack of goodwill but to a failure
in spiritual discernment. He later said that the delegates
accepted the pope's decision without rancor and that this was
one of the most beautiful examples of total obedience in the
Society.[128] In an exchange of letters, he apologized to Paul VI
for the pain caused by the event and acknowledged that the
General Congregation had misinterpreted the papal wishes,
but he stressed that the Society had never intended to challenge the Holy See, to which it owed the greatest respect
and loyalty. On the final day of the congregation, March 7,
1975, Paul VI told Pedro that he was much comforted by the
good spirit in which the delegates had accepted his decision.
Thus ended one of the most difficult and painful chapters in
Pedro's relationship with Paul VI.

During his later illness Pedro was asked by Lamet: "Did
you sleep that night?"

> Yes, of course. I have always slept. I have never lost my
> peace. I have a tranquil conscience. I don't know if I may
> have made a mistake. God knows, and in heaven it will be
> seen, but I always did what I thought I should do before
> God, what appeared to be my obligation.[129]

Despite what must have been a humiliating experience, Pedro in his years of illness affirmed that he had always felt great confidence in relating with Paul VI because he felt that the pope loved the Society, that he was an intellectual man and very interested in culture. Pedro's twenty-seven years in Japan and his worldwide travels on behalf of the emerging province of Japan had left him unskilled in the diplomacy of the Vatican: he had missed the warning signals that many of us across the Society had picked up at the time. Pedro had presumed that the Vatican would have been willing to explore the pros and cons of the grades issue before deciding against it—a naïve expectation, as it turned out. Significantly, however, after several months of anxious waiting by Arrupe, Pope Paul VI gave approval to the Congregation's decrees, including the central one on the promotion of faith and justice.

When John Paul II became pope in 1978, he would have inherited the criticisms already made against the Jesuits, and these were likely magnified as Jesuits began to implement the decrees of the 32nd General Congregation. The pope may also have believed, in common with others, that the Jesuits had disobeyed Pope Paul VI at the General Congregation. Arrupe, however, wrote to Pope John Paul II a spirited defense of the Society on the matter.

## In the Eye of the Storm

Excesses and failures accompanied well-intentioned Jesuit efforts to serve the cause of justice. A few of the more radical members threw caution to the wind in poorly made decisions. They ignored the admonitions of their local bishops, leading to accusations that they were rushing ahead of the Church and that in serving justice they were forgetting the service of faith.

Other Jesuits clung to the works at which they had spent a lifetime's toil. They were confused by this novel call to "promote justice," which they felt was the task of the laity. God's grace, they believed, had to do with preparing souls for the next life rather than trying to set things right here on this passing earth. The prayer for the grace "to despise the things of earth and love the things of heaven" was still part of the liturgy at the time. The great majority, however, rallied to Arrupe as the man who was interpreting rightly the values of the Gospels and rekindling the spirit of Ignatius.

Presuming the best of everyone, Pedro had pushed ahead with the implementation of the Vatican Council's agenda without catching on to coded signals from the Vatican urging caution. The issue of grades, as we have seen, illustrates this shortcoming in his style but also highlights his capacity to deal with negativity and setbacks: he never became defensive but instead remained focused on the truth of an issue.

A charming incident illustrating his optimistic style is related in which Pope Paul VI summoned Arrupe and read him a carefully prepared letter with twelve points, of which the first eleven were commendatory. The twelfth carried a strong admonition that the pope, with Vatican tact and diplomacy, was trying to get across. But Pedro, on returning home to the Jesuit curia, announced happily to his brethren: "The Holy Father has praised our work on eleven points: only on the twelfth did he show reserve!"[130]

## Spanish Jesuits

With departures of Jesuits rising to a thousand per year, Spanish Jesuits especially were critical of Arrupe. Many felt that his style of government was inadequate to the challenges he faced, that his tendency to believe the best of everyone was naïve. He needed, they argued, to face abuses with a firm hand rather than persuasion, to call his troops to order and discipline the rebellious. But this was not in Pedro's character.

Many were outraged by the practical outcomes of the new emphasis on justice. In the United States, Daniel Berrigan was protesting against nuclear armaments; John McNeill was writing *The Church and the Homosexual* (1976); Robert Drinan was becoming a congressman; John McLaughlin was running for the US Senate as a Republican and during his campaign remarked that "ecclesiastical politics make civil politics look like child's play." Fr. Arrupe's critics held that he should face such men with the ultimatum of submission or departure. Later the Spaniards would find pope John Paul II on their side: in 1980 he unequivocally demanded that all priests withdraw from electoral politics.

## "Turn Back the Clock!"

What, asked these critics, will happen next? They yearned for the old life, despite its rigors, its discipline, and its predictability. In the regularity of their religious life they could pray, do their work, and find security. When a group of them came to feel in all good conscience that they should break away to restore the "old" Society, Pope Paul VI took this group seriously but first checked with the Spanish bishops. He followed their perhaps surprising advice, which was, "Don't change!" Arrupe faced this group, humble though unafraid, but he had to work hard to commend to them the authenticity of the new forms of Jesuit life, which were intended to help the members deal with a different world from the one they had known.

The discontent smoldered on: "One Basque founded the Society of Jesus; another is destroying it." Three anonymous Jesuits stated in an interview that Arrupe was incapable of governing the Society, was oblivious to its ruin and deaf to the pope's warnings. But secession was averted, and according to Lamet, many of the most recalcitrant Jesuits, while remaining critical of Arrupe's style of governance, came to appreciate his formidable moral and Christian authority.[131]

Pedro in fact lived often in the anguish of self-doubt but found his confidence in God. Those around him came to know of his inner suffering when he advised them to expect it in their own lives. He had anticipated great suffering in acting out of fidelity to the Ignatian vision and was prepared to endure much contradiction, as is the common lot of prophets.

In Arrupe's way of proceeding, the gospel, the signs of the times, and the promptings of God experienced in prayer were critical. He worked toward decisions, not from abstract principles but from experienced reality and by dialogue. He respected ecclesial authority, submitted his proposals, and then humbly left them to be fulfilled in God's own time. His commitment to the ideals of Vatican II was unequaled: his successor spoke of him as its faithful witness:

> Some might call him a utopian dreamer, while others might refer to him as a mystic and prophet for our times. Still others might recognize him as one who has done many new things in the spirit of the Lord who declares: "Behold, I make all things new" (Rev. 21:5). This is what most characterizes the figure and the message of Father Pedro Arrupe.[132]

The renewal of the Society, in Arrupe's understanding, had to come in graced fashion from God; hence, his limitless respect for those who found it hard to envision or accept the needed conversion of heart and mind. He saw that the true Jesuit charism had become trapped in a rationalist understanding that had suppressed its affective side, such that instead of a mutual engagement by superior and subject in prayerful searching for God's will, obedience had become largely a matter of assignment to mission. Pedro's personal capacity for friendship, his interest in what was going on in people, his trust in allowing a man to make the final decision—such qualities restored the affective and emotional side of Jesuit spirituality. His loyalty to his men begot a responding loyalty, and obedience at its best became, for those of us who lived through his generalate, a loving expression of availability.

## Graced Conflict?

The neuralgic issues of Arrupe's years included that of justice in the world, liberation theology, liturgical renewal, ecumenical relations, mandatory priestly celibacy, birth control, and more. Unfortunately for the protagonists, the art of graced conflict was sometimes poorly understood and practiced in the Church. It is significant that in John O'Malley's magisterial work, *What Happened at Vatican II*, neither the word *conflict* nor *disagreement* is listed in the index, even though, as he illustrates, every other clause in its many decrees was fought over. The Church badly needed a graced way of proceeding that would transcend principled disagreement, but this was never worked through. The post-Reformation nugget of wisdom that "in necessary matters there must be unity; in doubtful ones, liberty; and in all things, charity" could have created a platform for open dialogue, but this must await the emergence of a truly synodal Church.

# 12

# POPE JOHN PAUL II

## A Singular Figure

Pope John Paul II shaped the Church for more than a quarter century, deeply influenced the political world of his time, and played a significant role in the Arrupe story. A short sketch of this controversial world figure is helpful for understanding the drama of Pedro's final years.

Paul VI died in 1978, and his successor, John Paul I, died after thirty-three days in office. John Paul II, from Poland, had been favored by a number of the cardinals at the previous conclave and became the first non-Italian pope in 455 years. He reigned for twenty-six years, from 1978 to 2005. An imposing presence, a man of courage with a wide vision, immense energy, and a willingness to address every issue that arose, he saw himself as a pastor of the world and traveled extensively. His writings include fourteen encyclicals plus works on philosophy, theology, and spirituality. He engaged skillfully in politics, stood by the Polish trade union Solidarity in its struggles, and is credited with the implosion of communism, although he himself protested that "he only gave the tree a good shake." He canonized more people than any other pope—475 in all—choosing them from many walks of life to illustrate the universal call to holiness. He led the Church through the beginning of the third millennium, in preparation for which he proposed an examination of conscience for the Church especially in regard to ecumenism, pursuing this in the face of strong resistance from the Vatican.

## Selective Freedom?

John Paul II championed religious freedom and freedom of conscience across the world, but he sometimes kept a tight rein on those within the Church who seemed to him to be freethinkers. He appointed Joseph Ratzinger, later Pope Benedict XVI, to head up the Congregation for the Doctrine of the Faith, which led to the silencing of many theologians who were deemed to have crossed the official line. He emphasized continuity in any interpretation of Vatican II and was cautious of episcopal collegiality. In the choice of candidates for bishoprics, it was said, a safe pair of hands was a prerequisite.

Some bishops came to feel that they had become mere delegates of the curia. Dedicated people such as Cecil McGarry, SJ, a close assistant of Arrupe from 1974 to 1983, asked:

> How can one continue to feel with the Church and to love it, as Jesuits should, when the Spirit of Jesus seems to have been arrested, as Jesus himself was in his time? How do I continue to love this Church? Many of the most burning issues are resolutely excluded by papal authority from the agendas of synods of bishops. Are the bishops not to be trusted? What is the true meaning of collegiality: should we not search for truth, wherever it leads, confident that it will set us free? I mean the truth about the place of women in the Church, obligatory celibacy, sexual morality, and so forth. Is open dialogue, so treasured by the early Church and by Vatican II, to be entirely abandoned? Why do those in power believe no longer in the guidance of the Holy Spirit, but only in that of central authority?[133]

The Jesuit cardinal Carlo Martini in Milan would declare shortly before his death in 2012 that despite the forward thrust of Vatican II, the Church remained two hundred years out of date. The Church, he said, is tired: our European culture is aged, our Churches are large, but like our religious houses, they are empty; the Church's bureaucratic apparatus is growing, our rites and vestments are pompous; the Church needs to acknowledge its mistakes and undertake a radical transformation.

It must be noted that Pope John Paul himself had asked for help in the reform of the papacy. He let it be known early on that he would not act as chief executive officer for the Italian Church but would instead exercise his primacy as a universal evangelist. He passed care of the local Church to the Italian bishops, but the universal collegiality promised by the Second Vatican Council failed to materialize; dialogue was in short supply, and the pope was also open to complaints by bishops and disaffected Jesuits to the effect that the Jesuit general was presiding over the disruption of the Church.

## Creativity or Fidelity?

Thus the tension between the Vatican and the Jesuits continued: the latter were laboring to serve an emerging world by implementing Vatican II with what they termed *creative fidelity*, whereas John Paul II, respecting tradition, was trying to hold the Church together in the wake of the Second Vatican Council. He was uncomfortable in having to deal with the unknown and preferred to see the end point before setting out on an enterprise. Both sides could appeal to the text of the council's documents, but because these had been drafted with a degree of compromise to secure their approval, they allowed for ambiguous interpretation. While most Jesuits believed that they were acting in the spirit of Vatican II, their opponents argued the opposite.

Arrupe's devotion to Pope John Paul II was never in question. But the two men were far apart in character and style: they seemed to see the world from contrasting perspectives, and common ground between them proved too small to allow for creative maneuver. The pope could be firm, unyielding, and authoritarian in the eyes of some, to the point of stifling freedom of expression. Unfamiliar with the dynamics of active religious congregations, he found it hard to deal with a man like Pedro, who was highly imaginative, made decisions through dialogue and discernment, and had high respect for personal freedom, intervening definitively only in extreme situations. In the eyes of the pope, Arrupe did not deliver what was asked of him: he was not authoritative enough in stamping out abuses. Given the pope's struggle against communism in Europe, it was not surprising that one of the neuralgic tensions between them was liberation theology.

## Liberation Theology

Liberation theology had begun in Latin America after Vatican II: it focused the gospel on the exploitation of the poor and the concentration of immense wealth in the hands of a tiny minority, of whom many were Catholic and enjoyed the support of members of the hierarchy. A meeting of Latin American bishops and theologians in 1968 in Medellín, Colombia, was addressed by Arrupe, who spoke in favor of liberation theology and the preferential option for the poor. Shortly after the Medellín meeting, however, some Jesuits, together with highly placed ecclesiastics, accused some proponents of the new theology of being influenced by Marxism, which was not entirely unfair. They argued that under Arrupe's leadership, the Society had lost its bearings by taking the lead in this dangerous and even unorthodox theological movement. However, Pedro presented a nuanced approach to the issue in a letter addressed first of all to the provincials of Latin America:

> Marxist analysis . . . implies . . . a concept of human history in contradiction with the Christian view of man and society, and leading to strategies which threaten Christian values and attitudes . . . Christians who have for a time attempted to adopt Marxist analysis and praxis, have confessed that they have been led bit by bit to accept any means to justify the end . . . To adopt therefore . . . Marxist analysis as a whole is something we cannot accept.[134]

## Submission of Resignation

Although the reign of Pope John Paul I was brief, within that time he was already preparing to deliver a critical address, perhaps drafted by Paul VI, to the Jesuit Congregation of Procurators. Arrupe asked John Paul II for a copy of that address, and the pope gave it to him with the sobering comment that he himself endorsed its tone.

The text praises the past labors of the Society and its prompt obedience to the Holy See, and it notes Paul VI's affection for the Society. It then lists a number of issues of concern: confusion between priestly tasks and those of the laity, which led to the neglect of the primary mission of evangelization; failure to adhere to the magisterium, which led to secularization and confusion among laity; and decline in the asceticism proper to religious life. Superiors, it said, should lead the order's process of reform by fulfilling their responsibilities paternally but firmly. The document ends with a message of goodwill and a plea for the Society's loyalty to the Church as shown in the past: its members must follow the example of the Jesuit saints and be contemplative in action while active in contemplation, as Ignatius was.[135]

In September 1979 Pedro invited Pope John Paul II to address a meeting of Jesuit conference presidents. The new pope's opening words were brief, and the reaction was shock when he said that he wanted to tell the Jesuits that they were a matter of concern to his predecessors, and likewise to the pope who was talking to them. He went on:

> Be fully faithful to the supreme magisterium of the Church and the Roman pontiff . . . and exercise the apostolate that is proper to an order of priests . . . even in the most varied and difficult of endeavours.[136]

Arrupe took these admonitions to heart. From June 1979 he had been pondering his future and discussing it with his advisers. On July 3, 1980, he wrote to his provincials to say that he had taken the first steps toward offering his resignation on grounds of age. He was then only seventy-three, but as far back as his election in 1965, he had argued that a general could rightly retire if he no longer had the vitality for his task. This was the official explanation of his decision, and it was supported by those whom he had to consult on the matter. He offered his resignation to Pope John Paul II; Arrupe was the first of the twenty-eight Jesuit generals since 1540 to take such a step. The Jesuit *Constitutions* would require the convoking of a general congregation to deal with the matter.

In a brief audience granted to Arrupe on April 18, 1980, the pope asked: "What can I do in this process?" Pedro replied, "Whatever you wish, because you are our superior." The pope commented: "Good." He continued: "Suppose I say no: do you think the Society will obey me?" Pedro responded, "Of course, Your Holiness." The pope seemed worried: "You leave, but I remain here: what am I to do with the Society?"[137] It seems that the calling of a general congregation had too uncertain an outcome for him, so he procrastinated, asking Pedro to await his answer and to continue in office for the time being. On May 1 the pope wrote Pedro a letter asking that for the good of the Society and of the Church he not resign or call a Congregation. He promised that their dialogue would continue.

# 13

## THE LAST ACT

### The Jesuit Refugee Service

The year 1980 was especially difficult for Arrupe, but he never lost heart. This may seem so obvious as to pass unnoticed, but it says much about his spirit. He was besieged with problems on every side, both from within the order and from within the Church at its highest levels. Moreover, the sorry state of world affairs must have been deeply challenging to a personality optimistic by nature. But he labored on, a figure of hope to many and of irritation to others, a man full of creativity and leadership. A far-reaching inspiration, in November of that year, was his setting up of the Jesuit Refugee Service.

Traveling in the East in 1980, he was shocked at the plight of Vietnamese refugees, of whom two million were risking everything to escape repression after the Vietnam War. This was the largest exodus of a people in modern history, and the world was not prepared for it. It was another Hiroshima-like moment for Pedro. In his Ignatian response, he asked his famous question, "How to do?" He then appealed to Jesuit provincials worldwide for practical assistance. Their generous response to the crisis led him to think more systematically about how Jesuits and their coworkers could respond to the ongoing plight of forcibly displaced persons.

Because refugee crises can break out overnight, Pedro wanted his companions to be available at short notice to leave established apostolates and tenured academic posts in order to enter into solidarity with refugees wherever they were to be found. This was in line with Ignatius's call for his men to go where the need is greatest and where no one else is available. From his travels he had come to see that, of all the people in the world, refugees were most at risk. He used a favorite image: "To incarnate the Ignatian vision, we must get ourselves out of the concrete!" His appeal struck a chord: offers came in of personnel and money; lobbying began of governments and other agencies. That the response was so generous shows that his efforts to renew the Society were bearing fruit. He stressed that those who volunteered did not have to be high fliers:

We are normal in that we are not geniuses. Perhaps we have a few geniuses in the Society, but very few. Years ago it was said that the great power the Society possesses is its well-trained mediocrity! Real excellence lies in commitment to Christ. Everything must be done with great discernment.[138]

With the help of the British Jesuit Michael Campbell Johnson, Arrupe laid the foundations of the Jesuit Refugee Service (JRS) and discerned its threefold approach: to accompany, to serve, and to advocate for the rights of refugees and forced migrants. The JRS has become a dramatic symbol of what the Society of Jesus is meant to be, and it inspires courageous laypeople to abandon their comfort zones to serve the unwanted of the world, who currently number some seventy million.

## "My Swan Song"

Arrupe made an exhausting visit to the Philippines in July 1981, presiding at fourteen Eucharists and delivering twenty-six addresses, always with the same inspiring challenge about availability to serve the needy through faith and justice, in a way that is rooted and grounded in love. What proved his final exhortation was an impromptu address to those working with refugees in Thailand. In it he returns to his call for interiority and communal discernment:

Situations such as these are very difficult and complicated. Everything must be done with great discernment. It is not enough to have a great idea one day and go straight ahead and act on it . . . In Thailand you are in one of the hottest spots . . . Courage, please! . . .

I will say one more thing and please don't forget it! Pray, pray much. Problems such as these are not solved by human efforts. I am telling you things that I want to emphasize, a message—perhaps my "swan song"—for the Society. We pray at the beginning and at the end—we are good Christians! But in our three-day meetings, if we spend half a day in prayer about the conclusions we expect to come to, or about our points of view, we will have very different "lights." And we will come to very different syntheses—in spite of different points of view—ones we could never find in books nor arrive at through discussion.

Right here we have a classic case: if we are indeed in the front of a new apostolate in the Society, we have to be enlightened by the Holy Spirit. These are not the pious words of a novice master. What I am saying is 100 percent from St. Ignatius . . . There has to be a basic unity of minds for this new type of apostolate just about to be born. What we are going through here is the birth pangs . . . With this medical observation I conclude my talk![139]

We have here a perfect example of what Arrupe meant by communal discernment!

# Cerebral Thrombosis

He was speaking on August 6, the thirty-sixth anniversary of Hiroshima. The following day, August 7, 1981, on his return to Rome, as he disembarked from the long flight from the Philippines, his companions noticed something was wrong. Pedro was rushed to Salvator Mundi Hospital, twenty-seven kilometers away. He had suffered a massive stroke that left his right hand partially paralyzed and his speech severely impaired. The diagnosis was cerebral thrombosis: the left carotid artery was blocked by a blood clot. He could articulate phrases, but his speech coordination was awry, and he had lost his memory of proper names. He still understood the languages he had learned but could express himself only poorly and in Spanish.

# The Pope's Letter of Sympathy

On August 10, Pedro was helped to implement the normal procedure of the Society by which the vicar-general, Vincent O'Keefe, would govern the Society for the duration of his illness or until a successor could be appointed. On August 27, 1981, within three weeks of Pedro's stroke, Cardinal Casaroli brought a personal letter from the pope, originally written in Polish. The pope was still in Castel Gandolfo, convalescing from an attempt on his life on May 13, 1981. Vincent

O'Keefe was asked by Casaroli to read the letter to Arrupe, who wept several times. Unable to respond, he only said, "Non posso parlare" (I cannot speak). The interview, which lasted fifteen minutes, ended with O'Keefe asking the cardinal to bless the general.

Here is the full text of the pope's letter:

"Most Reverend Superior General of the Society of Jesus:

The news of your illness has caused me to be gravely concerned. Now the latest information foresees that you will be able to leave the clinic in the next few weeks, and so you will find yourself more or less in the same situation of convalescence as myself, here in Castel Gandolfo, after three months of hospitalization. During this time I have prayed constantly for the Society, offering to God my daily sufferings. Recently I have added a very special intention for you.

I cannot forget all the things we have discussed in our conversations together, especially in the most recent ones. We have a responsibility before God: a common responsibility and also a responsibility proper to each of us, you and me.

During my own illness I have always been comforted by the profound conviction that the infirmity itself, more than anything else, will serve to set the course desired by God. I am certain that you also will find in your illness a similar light.

I express my sincere hope that that the Holy Spirit will help us carry forward, in the way God wishes us, the cause that God has entrusted to our human weakness.

With my apostolic blessing.

Castel Gandolfo, August 27, 1981.

johannes paulus pp. ii[140]

This letter is warm and sympathetic, and it speaks of the bond established between the two men by common suffering. It also indicates that perhaps they had shared more in their short conversations than we know of. Its conciliatory tone suggests that if indeed Pedro had recovered, he and the pope might have related better, because all that Pedro had yearned for was open and frank dialogue leading to agreement on what best to do in his given situation, even if it meant his own retirement.

There was surely a warm response either from or on behalf of Pedro, but much of the documentation between the pope and Pedro is as yet still classified and unavailable.

## Marginalized

Three weeks later, on October 6, 1981, news came that Cardinal Casaroli would arrive at noon bearing another letter from the pope and that he should be taken to Arrupe's room. O'Keefe received the cardinal at the door and led him to Pedro's room. Casaroli asked O'Keefe to leave the room because he wished to be alone with Arrupe. In fact, Br. Bandera, Pedro's nurse, refused to leave when asked, alleging that he could not leave an incapacitated sick man alone.

The visit lasted only a few minutes and then Casaroli let himself out of the house. When O'Keefe returned, he found the pope's letter lying on a small table. The general was weeping. What did the letter say?

After sympathizing with the general's pain and distress, the pope referred to Arrupe's resignation and to his own earlier desire to prepare the general congregation together with Arrupe, which had not been possible because of the hospitalization of both men. He went on:

> Therefore, after long reflection and prayer, I have decided to confide the task to a delegate of my own choosing, who will represent me more directly within the Society, will attend to the preparation of the general congregation, which should be called at an opportune moment, and will jointly, in my name have supervision of the Society's governance until the election of the new superior general.
>
> To that end I name as my delegate Father Paolo Dezza, to be assisted by Father Joseph Pittau. More particulars about the functions of the delegate and his coadjutor will be indicated in a complementary document.
>
> I trust that the Society of Jesus will be able to recognize in these decisions a sign of my affectionate regard for your person and of my sincere benevolence toward the whole

Society, for I earnestly desire that its greater good redound
to the benefit of the whole Church, in which the same
Society carries out such a broad and diverse ministry."[141]

The letter ends with the desire of copious graces for Arrupe
and the Society of Jesus.

Thus the pope suspended the constitutional process of
the Jesuit order by which the vicar-general—at that time
Vincent O'Keefe—would have steered the Society into the
next general congregation. This move also invalidated Pedro's
appointment of O'Keefe as vicar, the last administrative decision that Pedro would ever make. Was this to be read as an
indictment of Arrupe's administration, or of O'Keefe alone?
Hardly the latter, since the pope could have asked Pedro
to appoint another Jesuit in place of O'Keefe. The pope's
chosen delegate for the Society, it appeared, must be a man
outside the Arrupe circle who would act simply according to
the mind of the pope.

How did Arrupe understand this decision, the hardest
blow of his life? Br. Bandera said:

> "It was a very difficult moment, but Don Pedro demon-
> strated what he had been and still was." Pedro had asked
> him to read the letter to him again, so that he could
> understand it more fully. Then he said: "Take me to
> Father Dezza." Bandera responded: "No, you are the gen-
> eral: Father Dezza will come here!" Soon after, Pedro said:
> "God wants it so; may his will be done." Bandera noticed

in his face a sort of transformation and heard him saying, "God has his ways. He is great." "After about thirty
minutes his face and his eyes became again as they always
were: he smiled with serenity and profound peace."[142]

Was this Pedro's greatest moment? It mirrors Ignatius's statement that if the pope of his day were to suppress the newborn
Society, it would take him fifteen minutes to recover his
equanimity before God.

## Jesuit Response

Across the world, Jesuits and many others sympathetic to
the order and to Pedro were stunned. The marginalization
of Pedro and his administration, which had come without
warning, caused long-lasting hurt and anger. The Jesuits
already had to dig deep to come to terms with a papacy that
had in May 1980 rejected Arrupe's request to be allowed
to retire. If that request had been granted, some wondered,
might Pedro have been spared his illness? Now it seemed that
the pope wanted nothing more to do with him. Pedro in
his dark days—and they were many—must have wondered
if all his efforts to implement Vatican II were now judged
worthless.

But the Jesuits bore the test with maturity, dignity, and
obedience: nobody asked to leave the Society because of the
pope's intervention. As it happened, I was, at the time, living

alone in Somalia on my JRS assignment with which this book opens. I had only fleeting contact with the outside world and went through the gamut of moods for dark times, wondering if the Society would ever recover, or would be suppressed as had happened before. I discovered later that others had shared the same fears. Mostly I grieved for the man I loved and respected, for his physical disability, and his humiliation in being so abruptly sidelined.

## Paolo Dezza

John Paul II chose an older Jesuit as his delegate: Paolo Dezza was eighty, had lost his sight, and had found Arrupe's style of government challenging; surprisingly, he was Pedro's preferred confessor whenever the general was in Rome. The pope had picked a good man for the task of steering the Society in this extraordinary period. With a gentle and firm hand, Dezza guided the Jesuits through two critical years and was able to quiet their worst fears, that of a second suppression. More importantly, as John W. O'Malley says, he was able to persuade the pope that the Society was not the hotbed of rebellion its enemies had suggested. Some of these critics had predicted that the papal intervention would spark a massive exodus from the Society, and they seem to have convinced the pope that he should expect that disastrous outcome. Nothing of the sort happened. In a little over a year from the date of his intervention, the pope gave permission for the convocation of a general congregation to elect a successor to Arrupe and thus restore the Society to its normal mode of government.[143]

# 14

## LIFE WITHOUT EVENT, 1981–1991

### The Duty of Suffering

So it was that after Pedro's sixteen tumultuous years in office there followed ten largely empty and silent years in the Jesuit infirmary in Rome. He could follow what was said to him, but he, who had been such a busy traveler and so articulate about the Society's response to global issues, was largely muted and confined to a single room in semidarkness.

Pedro's active years inspire many people, but his silent years also give strength to many whose lives have fallen apart and who find themselves lost in a strange and barren land. What can we say of such years? How was God working, and how did Pedro respond? Teilhard de Chardin speaks of the divinizing of our passivities—that is, of those occurrences that litter our lives and over which we have little or no control. All we can do is accept them patiently and with resolute love; it is thus that they are divinized. Writing of an obscure Jesuit doorkeeper in Mallorca, Gerard Manley Hopkins reflects on the hidden and silent mystery by which grace works in an open heart:

> [But] be the war within, the brand we wield
> Unseen, the heroic breast not outward-steeled,
> Earth hears no hurtle then from fiercest fray.
> Yet God . . .
> Could crown career with conquest while there went
> Those years and years by of world without event
> That in Majorca Alonso watched the door.[144]

Thus it was for Pedro: he struggled to accept the consequences of finding himself, as he said, "totally in the hands of God." We can believe that God's grace finds its way not only in fruitfulness but also in failure and inability, although its path is over rocky ground and hard to trace. Like Simon Peter, Arrupe was taken to a place he "would rather not go." Miserable his Gethsemane was, yet he found God there before him.

## Sickness as Gift

Reflecting on his own suffering, Pope John Paul II had written an apostolic letter, *The Christian Meaning of Suffering*, in February 1984. He may have had Pedro in mind as he wrote. With his central focus on the passion of Jesus, the pope weaves his thoughts around love, power, hope, goodness, and grace. Suffering, he says, can release love: through the cross and resurrection new light is shed on its darkness, which is brought into the dimension of participation in Christ's redemption of the world. It is suffering, the pope writes, that best clears the way for the grace that transforms our souls. God's power is made manifest in the suffering that weakens us and empties us of ourselves.

Whether or not Pedro had the pope's thoughts conveyed to him, he would have made them his own. He did not complain, and in the depths of his misery he held firm in the obscurity of faith. He would have recalled Ignatius's terse remark that sickness is no less a gift than health[145] and that Jesuits who are ill should try to give no less edification in time of sickness than they did when they were in health.[146] Peter-Hans Kolvenbach spoke later about the "duty of suffering" Pedro had had to undergo. In Pedro's case this was not merely an ascetical action but a relational bonding with his Lord. As a Jesuit making the Exercises he had prayed to be a loving companion of Jesus even in his passion. He had contemplated the struggle on Calvary between life and death; he had stayed at the tomb on Holy Saturday; and on Easter Sunday he had contemplated the Resurrection. In this context "the duty of suffering" was an act of loving companionship with his Lord.

Here is his prayer for compassion:

> Show me how you revealed your deepest emotions, as when you shed tears, or felt sorrow and anguish to the point of shedding blood, and needed an angel to console you. Above all, I want to learn how you supported the extreme pain of the cross, including abandonment by your Father.[147]

He would have drawn on that ancient tradition of Christian spirituality called the "Law of the Cross." In a study of this tradition, the theologian Bernard Lonergan shows how faith-filled contemplation of the passion of Jesus reveals to sufferers that their unavoidable suffering, patiently and lovingly endured, helps to redeem the world. The loving passivity with which Jesus endured the cross brought the greatest of all blessings to the world, and as we silently ponder the decade of Pedro's dark night, we can believe that it was a time of great blessing to the world that continued, unaware, around him. Perhaps he had a sense of this depth of meaning at Vespers when he prayed Mary's words: "The Almighty has done great things in me."

Pedro liked to read from Teilhard de Chardin, his near contemporary, who had reflected long on the mystery of dying:

> Grant, [Lord] when my hour comes, that I may recognise you under the species of each alien or hostile force that seems bent upon destroying or uprooting me . . . and above all at that last moment when I feel I am losing hold of myself and am absolutely passive within the hands of the great unknown forces that have formed me; . . . Grant that I may understand that it is you . . . who are painfully parting the fibres of my being in order to . . . bear me away within yourself . . . Teach me to treat my death as an act of communion.[148]

Another essential resource at hand was Arrupe's unquenchable hope:

> The feast of the Sacred Heart is a celebration of love, not of pain and sadness. Now we understand how St. Paul could say of the servants of the Lord: "we are treated as sorrowful, yet always rejoicing" and how they could feel "overjoyed with all their afflictions" and why as he says to the Colossians: "Now I rejoice in my sufferings for your sake." All this leads us to assume a positive attitude to the sufferings of the Cross, and our joy increases the more we share in these sufferings.[149]

And so it was, we may believe, for Pedro: an experience both of great joy and great suffering. In 1977 an interviewer had asked him, "How do you manage to keep on being an optimist?" He replied:

> Very simply. It is the theology of history, or more simply if you wish, it is faith and trust that not even a leaf moves in the world unless God permits is. We are in good hands. "All things work for good for those who love God." Certainly there are many failures, many infidelities, but by knowing how to read these "signs of the times" and learning what God wants to tell us through them, we can discover in all of them a message that, in the middle of its negative aspects, conveys a positive sign, and one that is in the long run constructive.[150]

There is a breathtaking quality to Pedro's hope as expressed here, and we can believe that it sustained him on his bleak and lonely journey home.

## "Everything Broken, Everything Useless"

Early on Arrupe endured intense sessions of speech and physical therapy. He put great effort into them and learned to walk a little, linked arm in arm with the infirmarian. But gradually his energy for these sessions declined and he became largely confined to his chair or bed. Br. Bandera spoke of Arrupe's joy and internal serenity and remarked that when he would go into Pedro's room just to look at him, he noticed himself becoming peaceful: "God had given him that charism of giving peace and spreading it." He stated that Pedro was easy to take care of and never impatient; he bore patiently all that had to be done for him.

But Arrupe suffered from depression and endured the melancholy of a sick person lost in emptiness.

> I am alone; terrible, terrible . . . I am no use at all . . . I was always a happy man, I was always content . . . I used to speak five languages, and now I cannot express myself in Spanish . . . Here alone with God, alone, alone . . . everything broken, everything useless.[151]

He would cry upon hearing of those who had died. When Bandera dared to ask him: "Are you envious?" his expression would change and he would respond, "Yes, yes."[152] When told of the murder of the five Jesuits in El Salvador in 1989, two great tears fell from his eyes, and he said, "They are with the Lord."[153]

Arrupe did not express even the slightest criticism of the pope. In the early days of his sickness, he used to go down to the entrance of the curia to greet the pope as he passed by during his audiences; but he confirmed with a gesture of great delicacy and simplicity and without the least resentment that the pope did not return his greetings. While he acknowledged that there had been difficult passages in relation to the Holy See, he always did so without resentment; jokes about the Vatican displeased him. He singled out Cardinal Peronio, who led the Vatican Congregation for Institutes of Consecrated Life from 1975 to 1984, as someone with whom he had worked very well as president of the Union of Superiors General: dialogue was easy, he said, and much good work got done. This led one of the superior generals to remark on how much he had himself done for religious life generally: without Arrupe, he said, the map of religious life would be configured in a very different way today.

## Nourishing the Spirit

Arrupe prayed the Rosary with Br. Bandera until 1985. "Now I have more time to pray. I pray the rosary five or six times a day." Until shortly before his death he would follow Vespers with great devotion, and while he sometimes cried from depression, he also shed tears of consolation, as on an occasion in November 1981, when he seemed to have a mystical experience, during which he repeated: "God, and Mary, the Mother of God, want it so." It seemed to Br. Bandera that he saw the will of God in his suffering and fully accepted it, and his love for Christ supposed and included love for his Mother, who places us with her son and is the Mother of the Society. Pedro remarked:

Love for Mary was first taught me as a child: it has gone on growing throughout my life, without losing its child-like character, from the time when my mother died—I was ten years old—and my father said to me: "Pedro, you have lost a saintly mother, but you have another even more saintly mother in heaven."[154]

According to the faithful Bandera:

The Eucharist was like the air he breathed: it was every-thing for him. He appeared to be beyond himself. His recollection was such that he was not aware of what was happening around him. At the moment of Communion, however, he would raise his head: he was there, awaiting his Lord. That was how it was every day, until the eleven days before his death.[155]

Other moments illuminated the darkness and brought him consolation, especially any signals of appreciation from the pope and visits from Jesuits or news of Jesuits working around the world. He could discern the level of sincerity in visitors who had never understood or supported him. He enjoyed his birthday party in November 1981 and could recall happy events from past years, referring to them as "very beautiful, very beautiful." He laughed in recalling his practice of Zen archery: the self-control, which is central to Zen, he said, had helped him deal with the trials he had in governing the Society.

He composed a homily read for him by Giuseppe Pittau, on May 27, 1982, during a Eucharist prior to the meeting of the provincials with the pope. It was the seventeenth anniversary of his election, and it reveals the vitality of his inner life at the time:

> In this declining moment of my life, I feel closer to the Lord whom I have served. I leave all my deficiencies in the infinite mercy of his heart, feeling sure of his understanding and love. In the long hours of my forced inactivity, I am able to contemplate unhurriedly my past and my present. I thus strive to cooperate with divine grace in the process of constant purification and conversion that I have repeatedly recommended to the Society.[156]

## Totally in God's Hands

His formal resignation as superior general on September 2, 1983, read on his behalf to his brethren at the 33rd General Congregation, reflects the indomitable spirit of a physically broken man. Already quoted, it is worth repeating:

> More than ever I find myself in the hands of God. This is what I have wanted all my life from my youth. But now there is a difference: the initiative is entirely with God. It is indeed a profound spiritual experience to know and feel myself so totally in God's hands.[157]

His final words were received with thunderous applause and with silent tears. Later came a carefully crafted but unequivocal approbation of the life work of the sick man:

> We confirm the Society's mission expressed by the 31st and 32nd General Congregations, particularly in the latter's Decree 2 (on Jesuit identity) and Decree 4 (on Faith and Justice), which are the application today of the Formula of the Institute and of our Ignatian charism. They express our mission today in profound terms, offering insights which serve as guidelines for our future responses: the integration of the service of faith and the promotion of justice; the universality of this mission; the discernment needed to implement this mission, and the corporate nature of this mission.[158]

In 1995 the 34th General Congregation further fleshed out the Jesuit mission by including intercultural and interreligious dialogue with the service of faith and the promotion of justice.

## Conversations

Conversations with the Jesuit journalist Pedro Miguel Lamet took place in July 1983 at Pedro's invitation and are detailed in the latter's biography of Pedro, who was enthusiastic about sharing his version of the events of his life and asked when the material might be published. One may ask why he wanted his experiences recorded: perhaps because he had a limpid personality to whom openness and transparency were natural; he loved to communicate in a nonpolemical way the truth as he saw it and to share his experiences of what he called "the marvelous Trinitarian love that irrupts, when it so desires, into the life of each person." Hence his very revealing conversations in early 1981 with Jean-Claude Dietsch that led to the book *One Jesuit's Spiritual Journey*. Like Augustine and Ignatius, Pedro wished to highlight not his own achievements but the workings of God in his life. Yet he confided to Lamet: "I cannot resign myself to the idea that when I die the world will go on as if my life made no difference."[159] He saw himself as a friend of this world, which was suffering from so much injustice, and that he had been chosen to change it for the better. He believed that his life could be summed up in the words "Thy will be done":

> That doesn't mean that I consider my life to be something extraordinary. What is extraordinary is that, even though I have often failed to orient my life as I should have, the Lord has continued to make possible his plan in my regard.[160]

Lamet states that, although Pedro was enduring great pain and was difficult to understand, he was otherwise the same as ever: sweet, slight, at peace, and as always there was light in his eyes and strength in his personality. A tiny incident is related that catches the pain of his forced inactivity and silence. A friend who had called on him said as his visit was ending, "Sorry I have to go now, Pedro."

"Ah, you have to go," whispered Pedro.

What he would have given to be able to say these words of himself!

## Reconciliation

A residual anger exists among some older Jesuits in regard to Pope John Paul II's brusque intervention after Pedro's stroke. But indicators are available that show a change of heart in the pope's attitude toward Pedro and the Society. Couched as they are in John Paul's style and in Vatican diplomacy, each can be understood, if not as explicit apology, then as symbols of goodwill and reconciliation. In evaluating them, Ignatius's terse comment can help: "It is necessary to suppose that every good Christian is more ready to put a good interpretation on another's statement than to condemn it as false."[161]

Pope John Paul II is perhaps not thought of as a man who would easily say sorry or search for reconciliation. But his was a multifaceted personality, and we have already touched on his apologies for the sins of the Church. These apologies were researched by Luigi Accattoli and reveal that by 1998 the pope had made ninety-four apologies: for the Crusades; for the Church's treatment of Galileo, Jews and Muslims, Hus and Luther, and indigenous peoples. He had asked forgiveness for the Inquisition, for Catholic racism and engagement in wars and injustices, for the mistreatment of Blacks, for the schism of 1054, for the sins of the papacy, and more. An example: in his *Letter to Women*, in June 1995, his apology stated:

> Women's dignity has often been unacknowledged and their prerogatives misrepresented; they have often been relegated to the margins of society and even reduced to servitude . . . And if objective blame . . . has belonged to not just a few members of the Church, for this I am truly sorry.[162]

In preparation for the millennium in 2000, as we have noted, he set out a remarkable program of repentance for the past errors and infidelities of the Church, especially for those related to ecumenism. He did this despite determined opposition from within the Vatican by those who held that the Church as such, being the "total Christ," could not be guilty of any sin. In a public ceremony, then cardinal Ratzinger, prefect of the Congregation for the Doctrine of the Faith and stern enemy of erring theologians, was assigned the role of acknowledging on the part of the Church "sins committed in the service of the Truth." This added a touch of irony to the solemn event.

Pope John Paul II is shown as a forgiving man when wronged: on December 27, 1983, as indicated in a moving photograph, he visited the prison where his intending assassin, Ali Agca, was to spend the remainder of his life. The pope talked with him and celebrated Mass in the prison chapel.

## "The Enemies Were Wrong!"

It is against this background, I believe, that Pope John Paul II's interactions with the Jesuit order in the final decade of Pedro's life are important and can be sympathetically understood. I have gathered together the indicators I have to hand: there may well be more. They may seem small to the pope's critics, but the pope was operating on a massive agenda, of which his relationship with Pedro Arrupe was only a small, though important, detail. George Weigel's massive biography of Pope John Paul II contains only a few pages on what was titled "The Jesuit Intervention."[163]

## November 1981

The pope attended the meeting of the Union of Superiors General on November 28, 1981, and mentioned Arrupe, who was still its president after sixteen years in the post. He also congratulated Fr. Dezza, who had just turned eighty. Dezza met frequently with the pope, who was very intent on receiving firsthand news of the state of the Society and who authorized a meeting of Jesuit provincials for early 1982, to accelerate the preparation of the 33rd General Congregation to elect Pedro's successor.

## New Year's Eve 1981

Annually on New Year's Eve the pope had the custom of visiting the Jesuit Church of the Gesù and meeting with the city government of Rome, but on that day in 1981, he wanted also to visit Arrupe personally. He had already informed Dezza of this wish. A photograph shows Pedro greeting the pope. Speaking as general, Pedro said: "Holy Father, I renew to you my obedience and the obedience of the Society of Jesus." The pope responded: "Father General, sustain me with your prayers and your sufferings." He added, "What we have talked about cannot be mentioned." Pedro's look indicated that the pope had made him extremely happy by his visit. Br. Bandera commented: "For Father Arrupe it was a marvelous encounter, though the pope spoke little."[164]

The pope that evening took supper with the community, but Pedro did not want to go to bed until he had left. At 9:15 he asked Br. Bandera to take him down to the front door so that he could thank the pope personally for his visit. The pope joked with him, saying, "At this hour, a sick man should be in bed." Br. Bandera concluded: "That night Pedro slept as he had never slept since the day he got his stroke. I had a hard time waking him."

After his visit on the same day to the general curia, which was relaxed and informal and included an exchange of gifts, John Paul II commented: "Just as I have been quite edified by the Society for some weeks now, so also I feel edified by this meeting today."[165]

After the pope's visit, Pedro decided to dictate a text to be read in the next meeting of the provincials, which took place on February 23, 1982. In his letter, Pedro affirmed that he was happy and content, that he felt the pope loved the Society, and that for himself the Holy Father's decisions and desires were an expression of the voice of God. He stated that the interpreters of those desires were Fathers Dezza and Pittau, in whom he had full confidence, and that he had told the pope that he was offering his life and his silence as the only thing he could do to help the Society to follow God's will. His desire was that the Society be ever more intimately bonded to the Church.[166]

## February 1982

The pope, having had supper the night before with Dezza and his assistant, received the eighty-six Jesuit provincials in the Vatican on February 27, 1982. He was positive, honest, and grateful, and with intense emotion revealed the following:

This situation, undoubtedly unusual and exceptional, has required an intervention, a test that has been accepted by the members of the Order in a truly Ignatian spirit. I had been led to believe that there would be a rebellion: this never happened. The enemies were wrong. Exemplary and moving has been above all, in this delicate contingency, the position of the Most Reverend Superior General, who has edified me and you with his full availability to the indications of his superiors, with his generous "fiat" to the demanding will of God, that was manifested in his sudden and unexpected illness, and in the decisions of the Holy See . . . To Father Arrupe, here present in the eloquent silence of his infirmity, offered to God for the good of the Society, I desire to express, on this particularly solemn occasion for the life and the history of your Order, the thanks of the Pope and of the Church![167]

The pope went on to urge the Jesuits to be faithful to the initiatives of Vatican II and concluded by giving permission for the convocation of the next general congregation, which, he said, not only would give the Society a new superior general but also would give the Society a fresh impulse for carrying out its mission with a renewed spirit, in line with the hopes of the Church and the world.[168]

## September 1983

The pope made an unusual gesture of goodwill toward the Society by inaugurating personally the labors of the 33rd General Congregation on September 2, 1983. He presided at the Mass, during which he approached Arrupe three times: to share with him the sign of peace, to give him Communion, and to say goodbye to him. In his homily the pope reaffirmed his affection for the Society. On the following day, Pedro was presented with a photograph of the pope inscribed with the text: "To Father Arrupe, whom I am delighted to greet here present with us. I recognize how widely acknowledged he is for having governed the Society by his example, his prayer and his suffering." Pedro kissed the pope's autograph.[169]

## October 1983

The pope's secretary had asked Father Alcala, SJ, about Arrupe's health. Alcala went to visit Pedro, who appeared quite unconscious, and whispered into his ear: "The pope's secretary asked me about your health." Pedro immediately reacted vigorously and asked clearly: "What did the pope say?" Clearly this meant a great deal to him.[170]

## January 1991

From 1985 onward Pedro's condition deteriorated considerably. As was remarked, "He cannot speak, but his life does."

On Sunday, January 27, Peter-Hans Kolvenbach, the superior general, informed the Vatican of Pedro's decline and requested an apostolic blessing for Pedro. The answer came immediately by telegram, and later that day the pope's private secretary phoned to say that the pope would visit the dying man to give him his personal blessing. When he arrived, the pope prayed in silence for a while and then recited with those present the hymn "Alma Redemptoris Mater." This, the pope's final visit, lasted about a quarter of an hour. Had Pedro been aware of what was going on, it would have been a huge comfort to him given his reverence for the papacy.[171]

## February 5, 1991

When Pedro died, the pope praised the deceased general for "his profound piety, his zeal for the Church, and his generous and patient acceptance of the divine will in his sufferings." He voiced his final and moving appreciation of Pedro at the funeral Mass through his representative, Cardinal Somalo, as we shall see.

Thus closed what we know of the process of reconciliation. Doubtless more will be brought to light on the relationship between the two great men when the cause for Arrupe's beatification is complete.

# 15

## DEATH AND BEYOND

### Worldwide Tributes

Until a few weeks before his death, Pedro had maintained fleeting moments of lucidity but then he became deeply comatose. On February 5 at 7:45 p.m., the final decade of a life of extraordinary dedication and generosity mercifully came to a close: he was eighty-three years old. The immediate cause of death was a violent and long-drawn-out seizure, which was heartrending for those present at his bedside. The heart that was wider than the world was at rest. The body was laid out in the curia chapel, and past it filed laypeople, cardinals, bishops, priests, and religious. Telegrams and bouquets of flowers began to arrive from across the world.

News of his death caused a profound commotion in Rome. The Italian president and the prime minister came to pay their last respects. At the funeral Mass, the pope's representative, Cardinal Somalo, one of Pedro's former critics, stated that the pope had wished to be represented at the celebration to manifest his warm and profound remembrance of Fr. Arrupe, and his esteem and unchanged trust in the Society of Jesus. Cardinal Somalo recalled Fr. Arrupe's spirit of obedience to the Holy Father and his openness to the needs of the Church and the world, and he testified to the pope's esteem for and unwavering confidence in the Society and in this man who was, as the *Constitutions* wanted him to be, full of great goodness and love in order to undertake great things for God's service.

Cardinal Somalo ended his remarks by saying:

> Christian hope promises that once again we shall meet the unforgettable Fr Arrupe, the good and faithful servant who lived his life solely for the greater glory of God, and who has gone ahead to where the love of Christ, which conquers all, transforms death into new life.[172]

At the funeral on February 9, 1991, the Jesuit general Peter-Hans Kolvenbach spoke of Arrupe's radiant optimism nourished by profound faith, and how he had addressed the crucial challenge of Vatican II, the appropriate renewal and adaptation of ecclesial and religious life. "He dared," the general said, "to abandon customs and habits in order to open the Society, by means of spiritual discernment, to what God desired of it for Christ's mission in the heart of our world."[173]

The funeral was referred to by Giulio Andreotti, the prime minister, as a "triumph in death." It was, he said, long since the city witnessed such fervent participation by the people, in their lively awareness of being before a saint who had left behind him a path for the future of humanity.

Fr. Kolvenbach depicted with emotion and vibrancy the qualities of the dead general:

> Neither misunderstandings nor criticisms stood in the way of his passion for justice or service to the poor, not even when false interpretations of his directives gave rise to abuses. Nobody has ever been able to criticise the generosity that inspired all his efforts. Whenever he was asked, "Where is the Society going?" Arrupe answered with disarming simplicity: "Where God is taking it." He enjoyed an absolute and joyous confidence in the Lord, and he knew the meaning of hope.[174]

When the hymn "Into Paradise" was intoned, there exploded in the Church a long, enthusiastic applause, which continued while the funeral coach bore him through the streets of Rome to the Verano cemetery, where so many Jesuits had been laid to rest before him.

In June 1997 his remains were transferred to the Church of the Gesù, the resting place of Ignatius Loyola and Francis Xavier. All was done discreetly to avoid offending the Vatican: John Paul II was still pope. A celebration was held on November 14, which would have been Pedro's ninetieth birthday. It was also the feast day of the Jesuit saint Joseph Pignatelli, who had bridged the gap between the old Society suppressed by Pope Clement XIV in 1773, and the restored Society of 1814. The general stated that both men had suffered greatly in their labors, and that Pedro's efforts to renew the Society in line with the dynamic pace of Vatican II had been met with the incomprehension of some and with painful interventions by the Church. Both men, he said, had accepted the duty of suffering with loving humility at the hands of the Church.

## Beyond Death

It is fitting to explore briefly Cardinal Somalo's comment that Christian hope promises that "once again we shall meet the unforgettable Fr. Arrupe." Pedro was not afraid to die and to meet the God he had loved and served so well. In his final years, he had looked forward to death, but more, to what would come after it. In *One Jesuit's Spiritual Journey* (1981), he reflected:

The entire book has been about the past. Thus it seems to me that this conclusion should have been written later, when the final years of my life would have slipped away. But at the end I will perhaps be no longer able to dictate my thoughts. How many years will there be, and how will they unfold? Death, sometimes feared so much, is for me one of the events most to be anticipated: it will give meaning to my life. It involves the entrance into an eternity which is both unknown and longed for: it involves meeting the Lord and an eternal intimacy with him.

Eternity, immortality, beatific vision, perfect happiness: it is all new, nothing is known. Is death a leap into a void? No, of course not. It is to throw yourself into the arms of the Lord, to hear the invitation: "Well done, good and faithful servant: enter into the joy of your master" (Matt. 25:31). It is to come to the end of faith and hope in order to live in eternal and infinite love (1 Cor. 13:8).

What will heaven be like? It is impossible to imagine what God has prepared for those that love him (1 Cor. 2:9). I hope that it will be a "*consummatum est*" (all is completed), the final Amen of my life and the first Alleluia of my eternity. Let it be done, let it be done![175]

G. M. Hopkins offers a poet's hint of the experience of dying:

> Across my foundering deck shone
> A beacon, an eternal beam . . .
> In a flash, at a trumpet crash,

I am all at once what Christ is, since he was what I
    am, and
This Jack, joke, poor potsherd, patch, matchwood,
    immortal diamond
Is immortal diamond.[176]

What was it like for Pedro, as he slept in death, to hear his name spoken, as Mary of Magdala did in the garden of the Resurrection? Did he respond "Master"? Did the Lord embrace him as Pedro shed tears of joy? Did he, like the tired disciples on the lakeshore, hear the invitation "Come and have breakfast"? And did he bring to the little feast the good things that he had gathered over his lifetime? Did the Lord share the meal with him in quiet harmony and ask with a smile, "Pedro, do you love me?" and was the reply: "You know all things: you know I love you"?

We can imagine that Jesus led Pedro Arrupe to the Father, who embraced and kissed him, wrapped him in the best robes, put a ring on his finger and shoes on his feet, then called for a feast with friends, music, and dancing. "The lover gives and shares with the beloved what he possesses," as Ignatius says.[177]

We can imagine Pedro clothed in the glory of the eternal love, radiating the transforming presence of the Spirit. Relationships are renewed as he meets family and friends, Jesuits, Ignatius, all the people of God who went before him. Among those waiting to greet him are the victims of Hiroshima, the refugees of the world, the Vietnamese boat people. And Teilhard de Chardin. And on and on—the communion of saints. The applause, like that given him on his retirement, is endlessly multiplied. Pedro, who so deeply trusted in divine providence, now delights in seeing just how unerring and wonderful that personal care has been, and he meets many people whose lives he has unknowingly enriched. His voice joins the greatest of all stories with its divine and human authorship. With the God of the galaxies he explores the mysteries of the universe, from the greatest to the smallest, and then hears himself called again to serve, from his new vantage point, the world he loved so much. "Enter into the joy of your Lord! I will place you over many things!"

# 16

# LEGACY

It is a challenging task to sketch out Pedro's legacy, but I propose here some categories for exploration.

## New Pathways

At his funeral it was said that he was a model for opening new pathways for humankind, a man to whom many peoples and nations are indebted. He invites us to see that it is within human history that divine salvation must be found, that faith is linked to historical events rather than being a theory or a formula. Contemplating the dignity of each human being, we are to build God's civilization of love.

# God Is Intimate

We will always need the witness of persons who are passionately in love with God's world. Pedro was such: won over by the love of God shown in Jesus Christ, he allowed himself to be led by the Spirit in his service of the world. The agenda of the three divine Persons was his too. For him the Church and humankind were not old but young, struggling to find their feet. That is why he was challenging, positive, dauntless, serenely hopeful that God can carry out his purposes beyond human hopes and dreams. Arrupe witnessed in an extraordinary way to the disturbing freshness of Christ, and we can apply to him the comment by Emmanuel Cardinal Suhard, archbishop of Paris during World War II, that to be a witness does not consist in engaging in propaganda, or even in stirring people up, but in being a living mystery. It means to live in such a way that one's life would not make sense if God did not exist:

> The world of today needs God . . . [and] the values of a higher order. The world needs models of life that give meaning to its existence . . . Finally the world has need of committed men . . . who know how to direct the world in its restless search for peace and fellowship.[178]

Arrupe accepted the risk of intimate collaboration with an active and toiling God: hence, in the phrase attributed to

Socrates, his life unfolded as "a risk, but a beautiful risk." "To love and serve in all things" was his goal, as it was that of Ignatius. His life is a paradigm of the servant-leader who believed that communal discernment is the way to discover God's intentions.

## Creative Fidelity within the Church

Any judgment about the generalate of Pedro must take into account his endless efforts to negotiate the shifting realities of the postconciliar Catholic Church as it endured the high seas of change. Pedro was inspired by Vatican II as few others have been: he has been called the apostle of the Second Vatican Council. His approach provides a beacon of light as God's pilgrim people reach out to an unknown future.

He chose to work within the clashing dynamics of institution and charism, and to move with creative fidelity into the unknown. Pope John Paul II gave his approval to Arrupe's efforts when he spoke on February 27, 1982, to the assembled Jesuit provincials:

> The Church hopes that the Society will contribute effectively to the realization of Vatican II and help the whole Church to advance together on the great path which has been set before us by the Council.[179]

He bore his marginalization and his stroke with serenity and unwavering obedience to the pope, saying, "This is the way now." It was the final statement of his desire to hold in tension ecclesial faith and gospel innovation. Ignatius's guidelines about "thinking with the Church" must mean participating in the task of thinking creatively together with the people of God—not slavishly following the tired thinking of the past.

## Openness to Unfolding Reality

Pedro was open to new experiences, however challenging—we can recall what he faced in Madrid, Lourdes, Hiroshima, Vietnam, and Thailand. He invites us to gaze contemplatively on our world and to respond rightly to its unfolding. Pedro's driving insight as general was that the Ignatian charism, refreshed and liberated, was fit for purpose in the face of the issues of his day. He was elected not as "a safe pair of hands" but as someone capable of leading the Society of Jesus into a new age. His legacy endures in many hearts and apostolates. Across the globe—and most importantly in its poorer areas—schools, educational centers, refugee facilities, hostels for the homeless, and so forth, have been named after him. The Jesuit Refugee Service now has some 1,500 members in fifty countries.

Pedro's holistic vision anticipates the concerns of *Laudato si*:

> We are all stewards of planet Earth—a planet to heal. Our responsibility is to tend its wounds. But healing will be superficial if the roots of infection are not explored, and as far as possible, eradicated. It is the human heart which stands first in need of healing. Only through inner change will humankind become whole and feel impelled to turn in compassion to a planet in need of healing.[180]

## Mysticism of History

As never before, our world needs people who respond to emerging challenges by asking, "What ought I do for Christ in this situation?" or in Pedro's charming phrase, "How to do?" Like him, we are to be men and women with and for others, no matter where it leads us. Pedro's vision has aptly been termed "a mysticism of history." In contrast to a mysticism of engagement with God alone, historical mysticism contemplates and engages in the chaos and messiness of concrete events and takes responsibility for suffering humanity. The driving goal of Jesuit education—"men and women for and with others"—offers an ongoing challenge to educators and students to put their gifts at the service of the world.

# Hope-Filled Prophet of the Twenty-First Century

Hope is the great Christian gift to an anxious world. Arrupe so lived it out as to lead a startled senior Jesuit to ask, "Has God as much optimism as Pedro?" Like God, he dealt in possibilities rather than problems. He was future focused and found that God was out there before him. With a heart bigger than the world he invites us to enlarge our own hearts and to share God's dream of an inclusive world order in which everything is shared and every need met.

There is no reason to believe that Pedro's capacity to inspire will weaken. He has well been called a prophet of the twenty-first century because his challenges retain their importance today. Among these stands out the commitment to the liberation of people through proclaiming the Good News and matching it with justice. Through his success in recovering the original dynamism of the Ignatian charism, Pedro has enabled innumerable people to live out their Christian lives to the full in the most varied of circumstances, because Ignatian spirituality is open to every emerging need.

## Pedro's Influence on Pope Francis

Pedro's connections with Pope Francis as a Jesuit illustrate his contemporary influence. Francis was born in 1936, twenty-nine years after Pedro: for fifty-five years they were contemporaries, and they shared Jesuit life for thirty years. In his initial years of formation Jorge Bergoglio experienced the same sources of Jesuit life that had nourished Pedro: the Spiritual Exercises, the story of Ignatius, and his spirituality. Jorge experienced the seven final years of the pre-Vatican Council Society, and from 1965 onward he was enriched by the renewal of Jesuit life and mission inspired by Pedro.

In 1974, when searching for a provincial for Argentina, Pedro chose to risk appointing Jorge Bergoglio, although he was only thirty-eight. Arrupe chose him again as rector of the Buenos Aires House of Studies in 1980. He would have known of Bergoglio's reputation: that he was tough on liberation theology and critical of an overliberal approach to Jesuit formation. But Pedro's choice was a sign of his trust in the man. What Bergoglio thought of Pedro's style and of John Paul II's intervention in 1981 is a matter for further exploration. Suffice it to say for now that Pope Francis is carrying through Pedro's vision of the service of the world and the Church in the light of Vatican II.

## Au Revoir

To return to my opening anecdote about encountering Pedro, what stays with me after writing about him are the following: his ever-welcoming smile, his intimacy with the three divine persons of the Trinity, his unbounded horizons, his capacity for friendship, his courage, his serenity and imperturbability, his trust of other people, his gracious resignation, and his quiet acceptance of his prolonged and devastating illness. I also appreciate his radiant and infectious joy, with its divine origin. As Aquinas said long ago: "Sheer joy is God's, and this demands companionship."[181]

I look forward to encountering him again.

# Postscript: "Fall in Love!"

The following reflection expresses for many people the essence of Pedro Arrupe's spirituality:

> Nothing is more practical than finding God,
> that is, than falling in love in an absolute, final way.
> What you are in love with, what seizes your
>      imagination, will affect everything.
> It will decide what will get you out of bed in the
>      mornings,
> what you will do with your evenings, how you
>      spend your weekends,
> what you read, who you know, what breaks
>      your heart,
> and what amazes you with love and gratitude.
> Fall in love, stay in love, and it will decide
>      everything!

Since it first saw the light of day, the author of this reflection was presumed to be Pedro Arrupe himself. In fact, it was written by his contemporary Joseph Whelan, SJ (1932–1994) of the Maryland Province, author of the 1972 work *Benjamin: Essays in Prayer*. But the story of the origin of the reflection does not end there, because the thought of yet another author may underpin Whelan's writing.

Bernard Lonergan, SJ (1904–1984), was a Canadian philosopher-theologian, author of *Insight* (1957) and *Method in Theology* (1971). He reminds us that we have in us the pure desire to know, which is actually a deep desire for God. If we cultivate it, this desire ranges through human knowledge and brings us to the reality of God. God's love is already poured into our hearts through the Holy Spirit, who is given to us (Romans 5:5), and if we become aware of this love, we fall in love with the God who already loves us. Being-in-love then becomes the meaning of our lives. Lonergan writes lyrically:

> Our capacity for self-transcendence becomes an actuality when one falls in love. Then one's being becomes being-in-love. Such being-in-love has its antecedents, its causes, its conditions, its occasions. But once it has blossomed forth, and as long as it lasts, it takes over. From it flow one's desires and fears, one's joys and sorrows, one's discernment of values, one's decisions and deeds.

The resonances between this passage from Lonergan's *Method in Theology* and Whelan's reflection are indeed close, and the worldwide popularity of that reflection has been ensured through its attribution to Pedro Arrupe—a delicate example of divine providence at work!

# Appendix A: Arrupe's Final Speech to the Delegates of the 33rd General Congregation, September 3, 1983

*While greeting the delegates Pedro was confined to a wheelchair and could not speak. His final speech was read on his behalf.*

Dear Fathers:

How I wish I were in a better condition for this meeting with you! As you see, I cannot even address you directly. But my General Assistants have grasped what I want to say to everyone.

More than ever, I now find myself in the hands of God. This is what I have wanted all my life, from my youth. And this is still the one thing I want. But now there is a difference: the initiative is entirely with God. It is indeed a profound spiritual experience to know and feel myself so totally in his hands. At the end of eighteen years as

General of the Society, I want first of all, and above all, to give thanks to the Lord. His generosity toward me has been boundless. For my part, I have tried to respond, well knowing that all his gifts were for the Society, to be shared with each and every Jesuit. This has been my persistent effort.

In these eighteen years my one ideal was to serve the Lord and his Church—with all my heart—from the beginning to the end. I thank the Lord for the great progress which I have witnessed in the Society. Obviously, there would be defects too—my own, to begin with—but it remains a fact that there was great progress, in personal conversion, in the apostolate, in concern for the poor, for refugees. And special mention must be made of the attitude of loyalty and filial obedience shown toward the Church and the Holy Father, particularly in these last years. For all of this, thanks be to God.

I am especially grateful to my closest collaborators, the General Assistants and Counsellors—and to Father O'Keefe in the first place—to the Regional Assistants, the whole Curia, and the Provincials. And I heartily thank Father Dezza and Father Pittau for their loving response to the Church and to the Society on being entrusted with so exceptional a task by the Holy Father. But above all it is to the Society at large, and to each of my brother Jesuits, that I want to express my gratitude. Had they not been obedient in faith to this poor Superior General, nothing would have been accomplished.

My call to you today is that you be available to the Lord. Let us put God at the center, ever attentive to his voice, ever asking what we can do for his more effective service, and doing it to the best of our ability, with love and perfect detachment. Let us cultivate a very personal awareness of the reality of God.

To each one of you in particular I would love to say *tantas cosas*—so much, really.

From our young people I ask that they live in the presence of God and grow in holiness, as the best preparation for the future. Let them surrender to the will of God, at once so awesome and so familiar.

With those who are at the peak of their apostolic activity, I plead that they do not burn themselves out. Let them find a proper balance by centering their lives on God, not on their work—with an eye to the needs of the world, and a thought for the millions that do not know God or who behave as if they did not. All are called to know and serve God. What a wonderful mission has been entrusted to us: to bring all to the knowledge and love of Christ!

On those of my age I urge openness: let us learn what must be done now, and do it with a will.

To our dear brothers too, I would like to say *tantas cosas*—so much, and with such affection. I want to remind the whole Society of the importance of the brothers; they help us to center our vocation on God.

I am full of hope, seeing the Society at the service of the one Lord and of the Church, under the Roman Pontiff, the vicar of Christ on earth. May she keep going along this path, and may God bless us with many good vocations of priests and brothers: for this I offer to the Lord what is left of my life, my prayers, and the sufferings imposed by my ailments. For myself, all I want is to repeat from the depths of my heart:

*Take, O Lord, and receive all my liberty, my memory, my understanding and my whole will. All I have and all I possess—it is all yours, Lord: you gave it to me; I make it over to you: dispose of it entirely according to your will. Give me your love and your grace, and I want no more.*

# Appendix B: Prayer for Beatification of Pedro Arrupe

Loving God,
Your servant, Pedro Arrupe, gave his whole life in
loving service
of the needy and outcast of our world.

He led the worldwide renewal of Ignatian
spirituality and discernment, and challenged the
Jesuit Order to promote a faith that does justice.
He urged people to become men and women for
and with others, and encouraged them to love and
serve in all things.

If it be for your service and praise, I ask you to
grant the petition I make in Father Arrupe's name
[ . . .] and so to hasten the day when his vision and
sanctity will be celebrated by all the Church.

This I ask through Christ our Lord.
Amen.

# Chronology of Pedro Arrupe, SJ, 1907–1991

1907: November 14. Born in Bilbao, Vizcaya, Spain, to Dolores Gondra and Marcelino Arrupe, architect and cofounder of the local newspaper. He was baptized the day after his birth.

1914: October 1. Began secondary school studies with the Piarists in Bilbao.

1918: March 29. Entered the St. Stanislaus Kostka Marian Congregation in Bilbao, directed by Jesuits.

1922: Began medical studies in Valladolid and continued them in Madrid, from 1923 to 1926, winning the Extraordinary Prize for Therapeutics. As a member of the St. Vincent de Paul Society he assisted the poor, the sick, and others in need. These experiences affected him deeply.

1926: The death of his father. Soon after, he traveled with his sisters to Lourdes (France), where he witnessed more than one miraculous healing and took part, as a medical student, in the verification process of one such healing. He would later say: "I felt God so close in his miracles that he dragged me after him."

1927: January 25. Entered the novitiate of the Society of Jesus at Loyola, Guipúzcoa, Spain, took perpetual vows after two years, and studied humanities for two years.

1931: Began his philosophy studies at Oña, Burgos, Spain, but with the expulsion of the Jesuits from Spain in 1932, he and his fellow students had to complete them in Marneffe, Belgium. It was at Oña that he had intense experiences of God, in one of which he seemed to "see everything as new."

1933–1936: Studied theology with the German Jesuits at the Ignatiuskolleg in Valkenburg, Holland.

1936: July 30. Was ordained a priest in Marneffe, Belgium.

1936–1937: Completed theology studies at St. Mary's College in St. Marys, Kansas, United States.

1937–1938: Did his year of tertianship (the course of spiritual renewal that Jesuits take after finishing studies and before pronouncing final vows) in Cleveland, Ohio. During this time he worked in the prisons serving Spanish-speaking inmates.

1938: June 7. Received his assignment to Japan, after persistently requesting it of father general for ten years.

1938: October 15. Once assigned to the Japanese mission, he traveled to Yokohama and Tokyo. He spent two years in Nagatsuka, Hiroshima, studying Japanese language and culture.

1939–1940: Began his missionary activity in the Jochi Catholic Settlement in Tokyo. For several months he was acting pastor in Yamaguchi, a town first evangelized by St. Francis Xavier in 1550.

1941: November 8. As a foreigner when Japan entered the Second World War, he was arrested and interrogated by the police for 33 days on suspicion of espionage.

1942: January 12. Was freed from interrogation.

1942: March 9. Was named master of novices in Nagatsuka, on the edge of Hiroshima.

1942: March 13. Became vice-rector of the novitiate and the theologate in Nagatsuka.

1943: February 2. Made solemn profession in the Society of Jesus.

1945: August 6. At 8:15 a.m. he witnessed the explosion in Hiroshima of the world's first atomic bomb. He organized an emergency hospital in the novitiate and assisted about 200 patients with basic medical techniques learned in medical school.

1954: March 22. Was named vice-provincial of Japan.

1958: October 10. Japan was made a new province of the Society, with an international character. Arrupe was its first provincial superior (1958–1965). By that time he had already traveled around the world several times, gathering Jesuits and funds for the mission. During his term the province reached a membership of 300 Jesuits from 30 nations.

1965: March–May. Was assigned to the preparatory commission for the 31st General Congregation of the Society of Jesus.

1965: May 7. The beginning of the 31st General Congregation.

1965: May 22. Was elected 28th superior general of the Society of Jesus on the third ballot.

1965: July 15. End of the first session of the General Congregation.

1965: October–December. Took part in the fourth session of the Second Vatican Council and spoke on atheism and the Church's missionary activity.

1965: December–January 1966. Made his first trip outside Italy as superior general, traveling to the Near East and Africa. Many other trips would follow.

1966: September 8–November 17. Second session of the 31st General Congregation.

1967: June 27. Was elected president of the Union of Superiors General (UISG). Reelected successively in 1970, 1973, 1976, and 1979, he retired in 1982.

1967: October 9. Participated in the Synod of Bishops, representing the UISG, and again in 1969, 1971, 1974, 1977, and 1980.

1968: August. Participated in the Bishops' Conference of Latin America and the Caribbean, held in Medellín, Colombia.

1968–1973: Was appointed by Pope Paul VI to the Congregation for Religious Congregations and Secular Institutes.

1973: September 8. Convoked the 32nd General Congregation.

1974: December 1–March 7, 1975. Presided at the congregation.

1975: Was appointed by Pope Paul VI to the Congregation for the Evangelization of Peoples. This was confirmed in 1980 for a second five-year term.

1979: January. Participated in the Bishops' Conference of Latin America and the Caribbean, held in Puebla, Mexico.

1980: November 14. Inaugurated the Jesuit Refugee Service.

1980: First trimester. With the approval of the general assistants and provincials Arrupe submitted his resignation to the pope, giving as his reason his advanced age. However, Pope John Paul II (1978–2005) asked him to continue in office for a while longer.

1981: August 7. Suffered a cerebral thrombosis upon returning to Rome from the Philippines and Thailand, losing most of his ability to communicate; his right side was paralyzed.

1981: September 5. Was transferred to the infirmary of the Society in Rome, where he would spend the rest of his life incapacitated by ill health.

1981: October 6. Received a visit from Cardinal Casaroli, who read to him a letter written by the pope, advising him that Paolo Dezza, SJ, had been named pontifical delegate for the Society of Jesus, with the powers of the superior general, until a General Congregation could be held.

1982: December 8. Convocation by Paolo Dezza of the 33rd General Congregation.

1983: September 3. The congregation accepted Arrupe's resignation as superior general: he had served for 18 years and 4 months, the last 2 years in silence and prayer.

1983: September 13. Peter-Hans Kolvenbach was elected as successor to Arrupe.

1985: November. His sickness became notably worse, with diminished consciousness and capacity to communicate.

1991: End of January. Close to death, he received the visit of Pope John Paul II, who granted him his blessing.

1991: February 5. Accompanied by father general and community members, he died at 7:45 p.m. Many people visited his chapel as he lay in repose. He was 83 years old.

1991: February 9. Funeral Mass in the Church of the Gesù in Rome, presided over, according to tradition, by the Dominican master general, and concelebrated by some 300 priests. He was laid to rest in the Jesuit plot on the Campo Verano.

1997: November 14. Transfer of his remains to the Church of the Gesù, where they now lie.

2018: November 14. Declared a Servant of God. Arturo Sosa, superior general, announced the beginning of the beatification process, with Pascual Cebollada, SJ, as postulator.

# An Eight-Day Mini-Retreat
## with Pedro Arrupe

During his first retreat after becoming general of the Jesuits in 1965, Pedro jotted down some retreat notes, intended for himself only. He titled them *Aquí me tienes, Señor* or "Here you have me, Lord." He made this retreat out of personal conviction and need, to process the new and awesome role that God was asking him to play.

The retreat you are about to begin follows Pedro's all-embracing desire to be available to God in every dimension of his life and can help you make that desire your own. You can be sure of Pedro's unobtrusive support as the retreat unfolds.

Overall theme: "Here I am, Lord."

# DAY ONE

## Theme

I am infinitely loved!

## Scripture

I listen to Jesus whisper to me: "As the Father has loved me, so I have loved you. Abide in my love" (John 15:9).

## Pedro's Reflections

When we hear these personal histories, we perceive that something is left unsaid in all of them because it cannot be spoken: it is a personal secret that even the person themselves cannot fully perceive. This is the most truly interesting part, because it is most intimate, profound and personal. It is the close correlation between God who is love and who loves each person in a different way, and the person who in the depth of their being gives a unique response, for there will be no other response like it in all of history. It is the secret of the marvellous trinitarian love that irrupts, when it so desires, into the life of each person in a way that is unexpected, inexpressible, irresistible, but at the same time marvellous and decisive.

## My Prayer

As two friends chatting with one another, I ask the Lord to show me how uniquely he loves me.

## Closure

Say very slowly the Our Father, as in the *Spiritual Exercises*.

## Be Contemplative during the Day!

As opportunity arises and in Examen time, muse over the reflection in the Postscript (p 213).

# DAY TWO

## Theme

Intimacy with the Lord

## Scripture

"Come to me, all you that are weary and are carrying heavy burdens, and I will give you rest. . . . [L]earn from me; for I am gentle and humble in heart" (Matthew 11:28–29).

## Pedro's Reflections

Lord, I have discovered that the ideal way of acting is your way of acting. For this reason I fix my eyes on you. Give me that sense of you, your very heartbeat, so that I may live all of my life exactly as you did during your mortal life.

Teach me your way of looking at people: as you glanced at Peter after his denial; as you penetrated the heart of the rich young man and the hearts of the women and men who were your disciples. I would like to meet you as you really are.

## My Prayer

As two friends chatting with one another, I ask the Lord for an intimate sense of how he lived his life, so that I may see him more clearly, love him more dearly and follow him more nearly.

## Closure

Say very slowly the Our Father.

## Be Contemplative during the Day!

As opportunity arises and in Examen time, muse over the reflection in the Postscript (p. 213).

# DAY THREE

## Theme

"Know the love of Christ that surpasses knowledge" (Ephesians 3:19).

## Scripture

"But who do you say that I am?" (Matthew 16:15).

## Pedro's Reflections

When asked in a television interview, "Who is Jesus Christ for you?" the question took Pedro by surprise, and he answered it in a completely spontaneous way when he said: "For me Jesus Christ is *everything*. Take Jesus Christ from my life and everything would collapse, like a human body from which someone had removed the skeleton."

"It could be said that every line of the Gospel, every word of it, is throbbing with the boundless love of Christ, who is burning with love for every human being, and who dwells in the innermost depths of our heart. So we can speak with Jesus heart-to-heart: he and we can listen to one another, feel for one another."

## My Prayer

As two friends chatting with one another, I ask Jesus for the grace to make him the "everything" of my life.

## Closure

Say very slowly the Our Father.

## Be Contemplative during the Day!

As opportunity arises and in Examen time, muse over the reflection in the Postscript (p. 213).

# DAY FOUR

## Theme

"Be transformed by the renewing of your minds" (Romans 12:2).

## Scripture

"I heard the voice of the Lord saying, 'Whom shall I send?' . . . And I said, 'Here am I; send me!'" (Isaiah 6:8).

## Pedro's Reflections

A novice once asked him, "How much time do you give to prayer, Father?" Pedro launched into a little homily on the importance of prayer for a Jesuit. But the novice was brave, and insisted: "Father, how many hours do *you* pray every day?" Silence. Then the reply: "About four hours."

"Please pray, pray much. The problems we have been discussing will not be resolved by human power. This is perhaps my swan song for the Society! In our three-day meetings, if we spend half a day in prayer about the conclusions we expect to come to, we will come to decisions we could never find in books or through discussion."

## My Prayer

I pray Pedro's prayer: "Grant me, O Lord, to see everything now with new eyes, to discern and test the spirits that help me read the signs of the times, to relish the things that are yours, and to communicate them to others.

Give me the clarity of understanding that you gave Ignatius."

## Closure

Say very slowly the Our Father.

## Be Contemplative during the Day!

As opportunity arises and in Examen time, muse over the reflection in the Postscript (p. 213).

# DAY FIVE

## Theme
The poor are the friends of God.

## Scripture
"I was hungry and you gave me food" (Matthew 25:35).

## Pedro's Reflections

I felt God so close to me, and I saw him so close to those who suffer, those who weep, and those whose lives are shattered. An ardent desire burned within me to imitate him in the same closeness to the world's human debris, to those despised by a society that doesn't even suspect that there are souls pulsating beneath such great sorrow.

Nowadays the world does not need words, but lives which cannot be explained except through faith and love for Christ's poor.

## My Prayer
As two friends chatting with one another, I ask Jesus to bring me close to the world's "human debris" so that I may carry the poor in my heart and serve them as he wishes.

## Closure

Say very slowly the Our Father.

## Be Contemplative during the Day!

As opportunity arises and in Examen time, muse over the reflection in the Postscript (p. 213).

# DAY SIX

## Theme

The Eucharist as cosmic love

## Scripture

"This is my body . . . This is my blood of the covenant, which is poured out for many" (Mark 14:22–24).

## Pedro's Reflections

At the top of Mount Fujiyama my mind was bubbling with projects for the conversion of the whole of Japan. Above us was the blue sky, below us eighty million people who did not know God. My mind ranged out to the Blessed Trinity. I seemed to see Jesus and with him St. Francis Xavier, the first apostle of Japan, whose hair had become white within a few months because of the sufferings he had endured. If I had known then how much

I would have had to suffer, my hands would have trembled as I raised the sacred host. On that summit so near to heaven I understood better the mission with which God had entrusted me. I could repeat with more conviction the words of Isaiah: "Here I am, send me!"

## My Prayer

As two friends chatting with one another, I ask the Lord that I may appreciate the transforming power of the Eucharist in our world and in myself.

## Closure

Say very slowly the Our Father.

## Be Contemplative during the Day!

As opportunity arises and in Examen time, muse over the reflection in the Postscript (p. 213).

# DAY SEVEN

## Theme

Trust in God's providence

## Scripture

"Do not be afraid; you are of more value than many sparrows!" (Luke 12:7).

## Pedro's Reflections

I have the impression that my life is written in a single sentence: "It has unfolded according to the will of God." My vocation to the Society of Jesus in the middle of medical studies that so interested me; my vocation to Japan which superiors denied me for ten years while they prepared me to be a professor of moral theology; my presence in Hiroshima over which exploded the first atomic bomb; my election as general of the Society—these have been quite unexpected and jarring events, but they have at the same time borne the mark of God so clearly that I consider them as those irruptions whereby God's loving providence is pleased to manifest its presence and absolute dominion over each of us.

I am amazed and grateful not only for the privileged moments of my life, but above all for the uninterrupted and immeasurable graces I have received each day during the course of everyday life.

## My Prayer

As two friends chatting with one another, I ask the Lord to show me something of the golden thread of grace that runs through my history.

## Closure

Say very slowly the Our Father.

## Be Contemplative during the Day!

As opportunity arises and in Examen, time muse over the reflection in the Postscript (p. 213).

# DAY EIGHT

## Theme

God is close in our weakness and infirmity.

## Scripture

"[The Lord] said to me: 'My grace is sufficient for you, for my power is made perfect in weakness'" (2 Corinthians 12:9).

## Pedro's Reflections

The feast of the Sacred Heart is a celebration of love, not of pain and sadness. Now we understand how St. Paul could say of the Lord's servants: "we are treated as sorrowful, yet always rejoicing" and how they could feel "overjoyed with all their afflictions" and why as he says to the Colossians: "Now I rejoice in my sufferings for your sake." All this leads us to assume a positive attitude to the sufferings of the Cross, and our joy increases the more we share in these sufferings.

Now more than ever I find myself in the hands of God. This is what I have wanted all my life from my youth. But now there is a difference; the initiative is entirely with God. It is indeed a profound spiritual experience to know and feel myself so totally in God's hands.

## My Prayer

As two friends chatting with one another, I ask the Lord to show me that when I am ill, helpless, or aging I am totally in his loving and caring hands.

## Closure

Say very slowly the Our Father.

## Be Contemplative during the Day!

As opportunity arises and in Examen time, muse over the reflection in the Postscript (p. 213).

# Bibliography

Notes: There is as yet no definitive biography of Pedro Arrupe. My primary source is the article by B. Sorge: "Pedro Arrupe," in the *Diccionario histórico de la Compañía de Jesús*, ed. Charles E. O'Neill and Joaquín M. Domínguez (Rome, 2001), vol. 2, cols. 1697–1705.

For a shortcut to the heart of Pedro Arrupe, see his *One Jesuit's Spiritual Journey*; then Pedro Lamet's *Pedro Arrupe*, and Kevin Burke's *Essential Writings of Pedro Arrupe*.

Accattoli, Luigi. *When a Pope Asks Forgiveness: The Mea Culpas of John Paul II*. New York: Alba House, 1998.

Arrupe, Pedro. *Challenge to Religious Life Today*. St. Louis, MO: Institute of Jesuit Sources, 1979.

———. *In Him Alone Our Hope*. St. Louis, MO: Institute of Jesuit Sources, 1984.

————. *One Jesuit's Spiritual Journey: Autobiographical Conversations with Jean-Claude Dietsch*. St. Louis, MO: Institute of Jesuit Sources, 1986.

————. *The Spiritual Legacy of Pedro Arrupe*. Rome, 1985.

————. *Texts on the Heart of Christ, 1965–1983*. St. Louis, MO: Institute of Jesuit Sources, 1984.

————. "The Trinitarian Inspiration of the Ignatian Charism." *Studies in the Spirituality of Jesuits* 33, no. 3 (May 2001).

Burke, Kevin. *Pedro Arrupe: Essential Writings*. Maryknoll, NY: Orbis, 2004

Carson, Rachel. *Silent Spring*. Boston: Houghton, 1962.

Coll, Niall, ed. *Ireland and Vatican Two*. Dublin: Columba, 2015.

Corkery, James and Thomas Worcester. *The Papacy since 1500*. Cambridge: Cambridge University Press, 2010.

Egan, Harvey D. *What Are They Saying about Mysticism?* New York: Paulist Press, 1982.

Endean, Philip, and Elizabeth Lock, eds. *Chosen by God: Pedro Arrupe's Retreat Notes*. Oxford, 2010.

Harter, Michael, ed. *Hearts on Fire: Praying with Jesuits*. St. Louis, MO: Institute of Jesuit Sources, 1993.

Hopkins, Gerard Manley. *"The Wreck of the Deutschland": Poems and Prose of Gerard Manley Hopkins*. Middlesex, UK: Penguin, 1953.

Ivereigh, Austen. *The Great Reformer: Francis and the Making of a Radical Pope*. London: Allen & Unwin, 2014.

———. *The Wounded Shepherd: Pope Francis and His Struggle to Convert the Catholic Church*. New York: Holt, 2019.

La Bella, Gianni. *Pedro Arrupe: New Contributions for his Biography*. Anand, India: Gujarat Sahitya Prakash, 2008.

Lamet, Pedro Miguel. *Pedro Arrupe: Witness of the Twentieth Century, Prophet of the Twenty-First*. Boston: Institute of Jesuit Sources, 2020.

Lonergan, Bernard. *De verbo incarnato*. Rome: Pontifica Universitas Gregoriana, 1964.

———. *Insight*. London: Longmans, 1957.

McGarry, Cecil. "Interfuse Interviews Cecil McGarry." *Interfuse*, Winter 1998, 21–29.

———. "Seduced." In *Call and Response*, ed. Frances Makower. London: Hodder & Stoughton, 1994.

McGinn, Bernard. *The Presence of God: A History of Western Mysticism*. New York: Crossroads, 1991.

Malloy, Richard. *Lonergan and the Roots of the Arrupe Prayer*. Web. http://ivcusa.org/wp-content/uploads/2020/05/ Fall-in-Love-Stay-in-Love-It-will-Decide-Everything.pdf

Merton, Thomas. *Conjectures of a Guilty Bystander*. New York: Image Books, 1966.

———. *New Seeds of Contemplation*. New York: New Directions Book, 2007.

Munitiz, J. "*Here you have me, Lord*"—*Aquí me tienes, Señor*. Way, 42/2, April 2003.

O'Keefe, V. "Mass of the General Curia for Pedro Arrupe." *Interfuse* (Irish Jesuit Province), Spring 1991.

O'Leary, Brian. *God Ever Greater*. Dublin: Messenger Publications, 2019.

———. *To Love and to Serve: Exploring the Ignatian Tradition*. Dublin: Messenger Publications, 2021.

———. *Unlocking a Treasure: Our Jesuit Constitutions*. Dublin, 2021.

O'Malley, John. *The Jesuits: A History from Ignatius to the Present*. Lanham: Rowman & Littlefield, 2017.

———. *What Happened at Vatican II*. Cambridge, MA: Harvard University Press, 2008.

Rahner, Karl. *Theological Investigations* VII. New York: Seabury, 1971.

Scally, Derek. *The Best Catholics in the World: The Irish, the Church and the End of a Special Relationship*. Dublin: Penguin, 2021.

Somalo, Eduardo. "Fr. Pedro Arrupe: The Final Salutation." *Interfuse* (Irish Jesuit Province), Spring 1991.

Stourton, Edward. *John Paul II, Man of History*. London: Hodder & Stoughton, 2006.

Vatican II. *Constitutions, Decrees, Documents*. Edited by A. Flannery. Dublin: Dominican Publications, 1966.

*WAY Supplement 2001/102: Christianity and the Mystical*

Weigel, George. *Witness to Hope: Biography of Pope John Paul II*. London: HarperCollins, 2001.

# Acknowledgments

My indebtedness to Pedro Miguel Lamet is immense, and I gratefully acknowledge it: without his detailed research on Arrupe's life in the Basque Country, in Japan, and in Rome, I never would have attempted the present work. I thoroughly recommend his portrait of Arrupe as "a witness of the twentieth century and a prophet of the twenty-first."

Thanks to the Irish Jesuit Province archivist, Damien Burke, for his unfailing availability in responding to urgent requests for information, and to my community in the Jesuit House of Writers in Dublin for their patient and discreet support while this volume was gestating.

Thanks to the Loyola Press team who initiated the project and artistically steered it through to completion ahead of schedule.

Finally, my gratitude to colleagues and friends whose infectious enthusiasm helped to keep me on track during the darker days of Covid-19.

# Endnotes

1. Arturo Sosa, *Cause of Beatification of Father Pedro Arrupe.* Letter to the whole Society, November 14, 2018.

2. P. M. Lamet, *Pedro Arrupe: Witness of the Twentieth Century, Prophet of the Twenty-First* (Boston: Institute of Jesuit Sources, 2020), 362.

3. K. Burke, *Pedro Arrupe: Essential Writings* (New York: Orbis, 2004), 61–62.

4. Lamet, *Pedro Arrupe*, 442, 436.

5. Lamet, 372.

6. Pedro Arrupe, *One Jesuit's Spiritual Journey: Autobiographical Conversations with Jean-Claude Dietsch* (St. Louis, MO: Institute of Jesuit Sources, 1986), 101.

7. Lamet, *Pedro Arrupe*, 372.

8. Burke, *Pedro Arrupe*, 201.

9. Gerard Manley Hopkins, *"The Wreck of the Deutschland":
   Poems and Prose of Gerard Manley Hopkins* (Middlesex, UK:
   Penguin, 1953), 12.

10. Burke, *Pedro Arrupe*, 65.

11. Burke, 104.

12. Pedro Arrupe, *In Him Alone Our Hope* (St. Louis, MO:
    Institute of Jesuit Sources, 1984), 52–55.

13. Arrupe, *One Jesuit's Spiritual Journey*, 37, 44.

14. Burke, *Pedro Arrupe*, 149.

15. Pedro Arrupe, *Justice with Faith Today*, ed. Jerome Aixala
    (St. Louis, MO: Institute of Jesuit Sources, 1980), 271.

16. Spiritual Exercises No. 15. Hereafter the Spiritual Exercises are
    abbreviated SE.

17. SE 184.

18. Arrupe, *One Jesuit's Spiritual Journey*, 13.

19. Lamet, *Pedro Arrupe*, 402, 432.

20. Lamet, 435.

21. World Synod of Catholic Bishops, *Justice in the World* (1971),
    n. 6.

22. Lamet, *Pedro Arrupe*, 435.

23. Cecil McGarry, "Interview," *Interfuse* (Dublin, Irish Jesuit
    Province), Winter 1988, 26.

24. *Constitutions* 809.

25. Lamet, *Pedro Arrupe*, 435.

26. Burke, *Pedro Arrupe*, 197–99.

27. Lamet, *Pedro Arrupe*, 372–73.

28. Lamet, 364.

29. SE 231.

30. Burke, *Pedro Arrupe*, 137.

31. Lamet, *Pedro Arrupe*, 464.

32. Burke, *Pedro Arrupe*, 13.

33. Lamet, *Pedro Arrupe*, 312.

34. Lamet, 333–34.

35. Thomas Merton, *Conjectures of a Guilty Bystander* (New York: Image Books, 1966), 153–54.

36. Second Vatican Council, "The Church in the Modern World," in *Vatican Council II: Constitutions, Decrees, Declarations*, ed. A. Flannery (Dublin: Dominican Publications, 1996), 163–282.

37. Lamet, *Pedro Arrupe*, 38

38. Lamet, 39–43.

39. Burke, *Pedro Arrupe*, 58–59.

40. Lamet, *Pedro Arrupe*, 45–47.

41. Lamet, 58.

42. Arrupe, *One Jesuit's Spiritual Journey*, 31.

43. Lamet *Pedro Arrupe*, 61.

44. Arrupe, *One Jesuit's Spiritual Journey*, 13.

45. Teilhard de Chardin, *Le milieu divin* (London: Collins, 1960), 99.

46. Thomas Merton, *New Seeds of Contemplation* (1949; New York: New Directions, 2007).

47. Pedro Arrupe, *Challenge to Religious Life Today*, ed.Jerome Aixala (St. Louis, MO: Institute of Jesuit Sources, 1979), 2.

48. J. Lobo, "Pedro Arrupe: The Second Ignatius?" *Ignis* (Gujarat Society) (2020): 32–33.r

49. Arrupe, *Challenge to Religious Life Today*,viii–ix.

50. Ignacio Iglesias, ed., *Chosen by God: Pedro Arrupe's Retreat Notes 1965* (Oxford, UK: Way Books, 2010), 35.

51. Lamet, *Pedro Arrupe*, 208.

52. Gerard Bourke, *Interfuse*, Winter 1998, 20.

53. Lamet, *Pedro Arrupe*, 127.

54. Lamet, 127.

55. Lamet, 118.

56. Arrupe, *In Him Alone Our Hope*, 93–95.

57. Arrupe, 97–99.

58. Lamet, *Pedro Arrupe*, 120.

59. Arrupe, *One Jesuit's Spiritual Journey*, 60–62.

60. Lamet, *Pedro Arrupe*, 479.

61. Burke, *Pedro Arrupe*, 56.

62. Burke, 57–58.

63. Jerry Rosario, "Pedro Arrupe: A Modern Missioner, Messenger and Motivator," *Ignis* (2020): 46.

64. Lamet, *Pedro Arrupe*, 18.

65. Lamet, 172.

66. There are many redactions of his account, of which the most complete is in *Recollections and Reflections of Pedro Arrupe, SJ.* Pedro Arrupe, *Recollections and Reflections of Pedro Arrupe, SJ* (Wilmington, DE: Michael Glazier, 1986), 22–39. Here I largely follow Lamet, *Pedro Arrupe*, 172–75.

67. Burke, *Pedro Arrupe*, 41.

68. Burke, 191.

69. Lamet, *Pedro Arrupe*, 222.

70. Burke, *Pedro Arrupe*, 166.

71. Arrupe, *One Jesuit's Spiritual Journey*, 22.

72. Arrupe, 22.

73. Arrupe, 41.

74. Inglesias, *Retreat Notes*, 8n10, 36.

75. Iglesias, *Retreat Notes*.

76. Lamet, *Pedro Arrupe*, 264.

77. Iglesias, *Retreat Notes*, 22.

78. *Constitutions* 812.

79. John W. O'Malley, *To Travel to Any Part of the World*, Studies in the Spirituality of Jesuits (St. Louis, MO: American Assistancy Seminar, March 1984).

80. Arrupe, *One Jesuit's Spiritual Journey*, 98.

81. Iglesias, *Retreat Notes*, 54.

82. Bernard Lonergan, *Insight* (London: Longmans, 1957, 733.)

83. Arrupe, *Challenge to Religious Life Today*, 4–5.

84. Lamet, *Pedro Arrupe*, 435, 441.

85. D. Lane, "Vatican II: The Irish Experience," *Furrow*, February 2, 2004, 67.

86. Iglesias, *Retreat Notes*, 12.

87. Lamet, *Pedro Arrupe*, 264n4.

88. Arrupe, *One Jesuit's Spiritual Journey*, 78–80.

89. Pedro Arrupe, *Letter to the Whole Society*, August 15, 1968, *Acta Romana SJ* 15 (1967–1972): 318–29. See also Lamet, *Pedro Arrupe*, 287.

90. Iglesias, *Retreat Notes*, xlviii.

91. Lamet, *Pedro Arrupe*, 317.

92. Burke, *Pedro Arrupe*, 171–87.

93. Burke, 173.

94. Burke, 181, 185.

95. Burke, 155–56.

96. Arrupe, *Justice with Faith Today*, 21.

97. Arrupe, *Challenge to Religious Life Today*, 191–200.

98. Arrupe, 193.

99. Arrupe, 200.

100. Arrupe, 172–81.

101. Arrupe, 205–8.

102. Lamet, *Pedro Arrupe*, 391.

103. D. Scally, *The Best Catholics in the World* (Dublin: Penguin, 2021).

104. Frances Makower, ed., *Call and Response* (London: Hodder & Stoughton, 1994), 71.

105. Irish Jesuit Province Archives, 1967.

106. Irish Jesuit Province Archives for 1971. See also Arrupe, *One Jesuit's Spiritual Journey*, 81–84.

107. Lamet, *Pedro Arrupe*, 351.

108. J. Munitiz and P. Endean, *Saint Ignatius of Loyola: Personal Writings* (London: Penguin, 2004), 63.

109. Lamet, *Pedro Arrupe*, 365.

110. Lamet, 441.

111. *Interfuse* 139: Easter 2009.

112. Burke, *Pedro Arrupe*, 201.

113. Iglesias, *Retreat Notes*, xvii.

114. Iglesias, 73.

115. Burke, *Pedro Arrupe*, 15.

116. Karl Rahner, *Theological Investigations* (New York: Seabury Press), 7:15, 11.

117. Pope Francis, *Laudato si*, nn. 84, 233, 236.

118. *Constitutions* 809.

119. Lamet, *Pedro Arrupe*, 361.

120. *Interfuse* 169; Easter 2009, 63.

121. Burke, *Pedro Arrupe*, 55.

122. Teilhard de Chardin, *Hymn of the Universe* (London: Collins, 1965), 19.

123. *Laudato si*, 236.

124. Synod: Justice, 6.

125. Lamet, *Pedro Arrupe* 336.

126. Pedro Arrupe, "Address to the Congregation of Procurators,"*Acta Romana SJ* 17 (1978): 541.

127. Conference on Commitment to Justice in Jesuit Higher Education, Santa Clara, 2000, 12.

128. Lamet, *Pedro Arrupe*, 335.

129. Lamet, 336.

130. Gianni La Bella, ed., *Pedro Arrupe: New Contributions for His Biography* (Anand, India: Gujarat Sahitya Prakash, 2008), 37.

131. Lamet, *Pedro Arrupe*, 300.

132. Lamet, 466.

133. Makower, *Call and Response*, 77.

134. Pedro Arrupe, "On Marxist Analysis,"*Acta Romana SJ* (1980): 342–43.

135. Lamet, *Pedro Arrupe*, 383–84.

136. Lamet, 393.

137. Lamet, 398–99.

138. Burke, *Pedro Arrupe*, 168.

139. Burke, 170–71.

140. Lamet, *Pedro Arrupe*, 416–17.

141. Lamet, 419.

142. Lamet, 419–20.

143. John W. O'Malley, *The Jesuits: A History from Ignatius to the Present* (New York: Rowman & Littlefield, 2017), 107.

144. Hopkins, 66.

145. SE 23

146. *Constitutions* 272.

147. M. Harter, ed., *Hearts on Fire: Praying with Jesuits* (St. Louis, MO: Institute of Jesuit Sources, 1993, 64.

148. Chardin, *Le milieu divin*, 69–70.

149. Arrupe, *In Him Alone Our Hope*, 114.

150. Arrupe, *Justice with Faith Today*, 271–72.

151. Lamet, *Pedro Arrupe*, 432.

152. Lamet, 424.

153. Lamet, 456.

154. Lamet, 30.

155. Lamet, 425.

156. Lamet, 430.

157. Burke, *Pedro Arrupe*, 201.

158. 33rd General Congregation, 1983: Decree 1, n. 38.

159. Lamet, *Pedro Arrupe*, 87.

160. Lamet, 456.

161. SE 22.

162. L. Accattoli, *When a Pope Asks Forgiveness: The Mea Culpas of John Paul II* (New York: Alba House, 1998), 110.

163. G. Weigel, *Witness to Hope* (London: HarperCollins, 2005), 425–30.

164. Lamet, *Pedro Arrupe*, 427.

165. Lamet, 428.

166. Lamet, 428.

167. John Paul II, *Discourse to the Fathers Provincial of the Society of Jesus,* February 27, 1982, in *Notices of the Jesuits of Italy* 15, supplement 34 (1982–1983), sec. 1.

168. Lamet, *Pedro Arrupe*, 429.

169. Lamet, 447.

170. Lamet, 452.

171. Lamet, 459.

172. Cardinal Eduardo Somalo, "The Final Salutation," *Interfuse*, Summer 1991, 10.

173. Lamet, 464.

174. Lamet, 461–62.

175. Arrupe, *One Jesuit's Spiritual Journey*, 102–3.

176. Hopkins, 66.

177. SE 231.

178. Arrupe, *Challenge to Religious Life Today*, 147.

179. Lamet, *Pedro Arrupe*, 429.

180. P. Arrupe, *A Planet to Heal* (Rome: Ignatian Centre of Spirituality, 1975), 9.

181. 1 *Sententiae* 2.1.

# About the Author

Dr. Brian Grogan, SJ, is a former president of Milltown Institute of Theology and Philosophy, Dublin, and is Emeritus Associate Professor of Spirituality. He also served as director and editor of Sacred Space, the international prayer web site of the Irish Jesuits. He has written extensively on Ignatian spirituality and has lectured and led workshops for many years. Currently he lives in the Jesuit House of Writers in Dublin, Ireland, and ministers in the Jesuit Infirmary close by.

AN EXCERPT FROM

# GOD
# IS RIGHT
# IN FRONT
# OF YOU

## A FIELD GUIDE TO
## IGNATIAN SPIRITUALITY

BRIAN GROGAN, SJ

# 1

# HOW GOD CAME IN
# SEARCH OF IGNATIUS

## Who Is Seeking Whom?

Seeking and finding God is not a new idea that began with
Ignatius of Loyola. We find it over and over in scripture. The
verse that comes most easily to us, perhaps, is from Jeremiah:
"When you search for me, you will find me; if you seek me
with all your heart, I will let you find me, says the Lord"
(Jeremiah 29:13).

But who first searches for the other? Originally I titled
this chapter "How Ignatius Came to Search for God," but I
came to see—or was brought to see!—that I had the emphasis wrong: God first searches for us. God's first word to Adam

is, "Adam, where are you?" (Genesis 3:9). The psalmist prays, "O Lord, you have searched me and known me . . . Search me and know my heart" (Psalm 139). The theme of God as "visiting his people" is strong in the history of revelation. It is fully achieved in the Incarnation. "He came to his own people" (John 1:11). In the resurrection appearances, Jesus is the one who takes the initiative in the encounters with his disciples.

And because we are creatures, seeking our Creator is a primary response of humankind and is the origin of the religious instinct. "The wise person rises early to seek the Lord who made him" (Ecclesiasticus 39:5). Jesus says, "Search and you will find" (Matthew 7:7).

## All Reality Seeks God

Searching for God is part of our DNA. St. Thomas Aquinas remarks that all created reality seeks God, by which he means that everything desires to continue in existence, and existence comes from God. Those wonderful people of 2,500 years ago who composed the scriptural Canticles had a deep sense of this. These songs ask all creation to "bless the Lord" (see Daniel 3:57–88, Psalm 148, and others). Sea monsters, mountains, trees, animals, heat, cold, and storm, kings and peoples, young and old—all have their role to play in the cosmic choir as it praises God. In this sense all created reality participates in seeking and finding God. When we are struggling alone to find God, it is encouraging to know that we are being carried along by this cosmic dynamic. Our need for God is not accidental to us but expresses our total reality. It can rightly be said that each of us *is* a cry for help, each of us *is* a need for God.

But back to Ignatius, who witnessed in his own story and his teaching how we can be helped to find God in a personal way.

## What Was Ignatius Like?

Ignatius of Loyola, 1491–1556, was, first and foremost, a real person; he was enthusiastic, alive, warm, and attractive, a visionary leader, capable and energetic. As his life moved on, he slowly became more reflective about what was going on in himself. He became a man passionately in love with God and the world around him. He came to understand that this world, which we think of as *ours*, is in fact God's world and that God is busy in it and can be found everywhere in it.

Historically Ignatius spans two worlds. He was born in an obscure place, Loyola (the name means "a bog"), in the Basque country of Northern Spain at the end of the Medieval Period. But he lived out his life in the world of the Renaissance. He was small, liked to dress well, and as yet did not carry the limp that resulted from a battle in 1521. As a young man he was shaped by the medieval traditions of knighthood and chivalry. Had God not dramatically intervened to beckon him in a different direction, he might have lived out the life of a conquistador and died violently and unremembered.

## Conquistadors

The Spanish word *conquistadores* means "conquerors." They played an important role in the Spanish and Portuguese colonisations of Central and South America in the sixteenth century. They were knights, individualistic, completely themselves. There was nothing of the "unknown soldier" about them. They had a passion for personal reputation and were full of prickly pride. They disliked discipline and regimentation and insisted on being consulted about every decision. On the other hand, they were totally committed to their chosen lord. This helps to explain their extravagant daring and their indifference to wounds, fatigue, and even death. They conducted themselves with the high seriousness of men conscious of taking part in great deeds.

Ignatius pulsed with the blood of the conquistadors. No wonder, then, that he was willing in 1521 to defend Pamplona, single-handed if necessary, for the sake of his lord, the Duke of Najera. The same year saw the fall of Mexico City to Cortes. Cortes had only a tiny army, but it kept together in spite of incredible hardships because of the personal bond between soldier and leader. Out of this period, then, Ignatius emerges as dreaming impossible dreams, single-minded and totally committed, with a conviction of his own importance in the scheme of things and of the rightness of what he was doing.

## Enter God

During the siege of Pamplona, Ignatius's leg was badly injured by a cannonball. He was then about thirty years old. He lay in bed for a long time and suffered much while it healed. He liked to read and dream of adventure, but, unfortunately, there were no interesting novels or adventure stories to hand; the only books available to him during this time were the *Life of Christ* and the *Lives of the Saints*.

Reading these stories, he slowly began to dream a different dream. He pondered on the purpose of life and found, to his surprise, that his allegiance was shifting from an earthly to a heavenly lord. In his own words: "I was like a man roused from heavy slumber . . . What strange life is this that I am now beginning to live?" Those around him said that he became "a new man with a new mind." How did this happen?

# Jesus Becomes His Lord

From reading the *Life of Christ* and the *Lives of the Saints* Ignatius came to see—with a shock—that God loved him and was personally interested in him. Being imaginative, Ignatius was able to enter fully into the scenes of the Gospels. He now saw Jesus as the true Lord, the one whose enterprise was truly worthwhile, the one who had suffered and died and risen for him. He became aware that God was *for him*, on his side, and had always been so. Overwhelmed, his initial response was one of gratitude. Why was God so good? But there was no answer. *There is no answer.* God is just like that.

It is consoling for us that thirty years of his life had passed before Ignatius began to engage in the mysterious encounters the human heart can have with God. Such encounters are intensely private and unwitnessed—and usually unrecorded. Yet we too can have these encounters because God meets us in every situation.

When Ignatius caught on to what was happening, he began to record his experiences. In his meetings with others he found it helpful to share something of how God was dealing with himself and how he dealt with God. But each life is unique, and Ignatius's gift lay primarily in his ability to enable others to enter a process of contemplative reflection whereby they could meet God directly themselves and come to understand how God was engaging with them in their own life situations. Recall the images of the sculptor and the dancing tutor!

Thus was born his little book called *Spiritual Exercises*. The exercises became immensely popular and are today more so than ever. This is because we all have to make decisions, and we want to make them well and find God in them. We will return to this topic later.

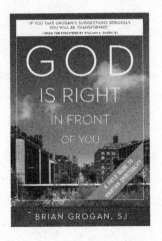

**Available online and wherever books are sold.**
**ISBN: 978-0829450224**
**$14.99**